# Classroom Activities
# For
# Criminal Justice

Edited by

## Laura B. Myers
Western Carolina University

## Larry J. Myers
Western Carolina University

**WADSWORTH**
CENGAGE Learning™

Australia • Brazil • Japan • Korea • Mexico • Singapore • Spain • United Kingdom • United States

**Classroom Activities For Criminal Justice**
Laura B. Myers,
Larry J. Myers

For product information and technology assistance, contact us at **Cengage Learning Customer & Sales Support, 1-800-354-9706**

For permission to use material from this text or product, submit all requests online at **cengage.com/permissions** Further permissions questions can be emailed to **permissionrequest@cengage.com**

ISBN-13: 978-0-495-10382-0

ISBN-10: 0-495-10382-9

**Wadsworth**
10 Davis Drive
Belmont, CA 94002-3098
USA

Cengage Learning is a leading provider of customized learning solutions with office locations around the globe, including Singapore, the United Kingdom, Australia, Mexico, Brazil, and Japan. Locate your local office at: **international.cengage.com/region**

Cengage Learning products are represented in Canada by Nelson Education, Ltd.

For your course and learning solutions, visit **academic.cengage.com**

Purchase any of our products at your local college store or at our preferred online store **www.ichapters.com**

Printed in the United States of America
4 5 6  14 13 12 11 10

## ACKNOWLEDGMENTS

The authors would like to acknowledge the support and inspiration of those who made this book possible. Thanks go to Rebecca Johnson, Carolyn Henderson-Meir, and Terra Schultz of Thompson Publishing who worked with us in the creation of this book. A special thanks to Terra for her educational inspiration that has led to great opportunities for criminal justice educators to share their love of education with other criminal justice educators.

Special thanks and appreciation go to the chair of our department at Western Carolina University, Dr. Ronald Hunter, for his support of this project.

Finally, we would like to thank our two children, Robert Ryan and Taylor Jessica, for their inspiration to create educational literature for other criminal justice educators. We love what we do and our children provide us the best model for being the best educators we can be. Their inspiration leads us to write about honing the craft of criminal justice teaching. The birth of our last child, Taylor Jessica, inspired us the most because her birth impacted our perceptions of higher education and those who serve as educators. Teaching is truly a moral endeavor and great educators are those who want to be the best professionals they can be. They are the ones who will read this book and use it to hone their teaching craft.

We acknowledge you, the true criminal justice teaching professionals, the ones who make the difference in the lives of your students and your colleagues. You prove it with every action and deed.

Laura B. Myers
Larry J. Myers

# TABLE OF CONTENTS

# CHAPTER 1

## THE USE OF ACTIVE AND APPLIED LEARNING ACTIVITIES IN THE CRIMINAL JUSTICE CLASSROOM

Larry J. Myers and Laura B. Myers
Western Carolina University

The traditional lecture in the criminal justice classroom has imparted a legacy of criminal justice knowledge throughout the history of criminal justice higher education. Topics such as criminological theory, police practices, court operations, and correctional history have been shared with students by instructors who wanted to educate potential criminal justice professionals about the wealth of knowledge associated with being the best professionals possible. While the traditional lecture has prevailed as a primary method for teaching criminal justice, innovative instructors have developed different methods for creating learning in the criminal justice classroom. Application activities have been invented by these instructors to find a more realistic way to teach criminal justice and to closer approximate the knowledge, skills, and abilities that criminal justice graduates will need to be competitive in the field.

This transition from the passive learning style of the traditional lecture to the active learning style of the application activity has involved a new form of learning that has created the potential for students to learn more criminal justice information, to retain that knowledge, and to use such knowledge in their future employment. Active and applied learning methods have a greater chance of creating the learning necessary to produce better criminal justice graduates. A comparison of passive and active learning along with a model for using active learning illustrates the need for using applied learning activities in the criminal justice classroom.

### Active and Passive Learning Compared

Passive learning created by the traditional lecture only requires the lower order thinking skills of repetition, memorization, and recall. Bloom (1984) refers to these lower order thinking skills as basic knowledge and comprehension. Tests created to assess knowledge and comprehension rely

1

on the cues of list, define, tell, summarize, and discuss. Such lower order thinking skills do not develop critical thinking skills or analytical ability. The higher order thinking skills of problem solving and analysis are not exercised or developed with the classroom lecture. Other classroom pedagogies are designed to create the higher order thinking skills of application, analysis, synthesis, and evaluation. The cues used to elicit such thinking skills include apply, solve, compare, integrate, and assess. The process of acting on material, analyzing situations or scenarios, and solving problems creates a criminal justice graduate with a higher level of cognitive development who possesses the skills necessary to act on their work in a manner that goes beyond the simple middle ranges of cognitive development.

The process of active learning can be explained with a model of active learning developed by Fink (1999). Fink's model dissects active learning into the processes of experience and dialogue. Neither experience nor dialogue alone creates the active learning needed to develop the critical thinking and analytical skills needed by the college graduate. Both processes must occur. The student must have experience by both observing and doing. Students must observe others doing the work of the criminal justice professional to absorb the processes and to learn the necessary methods and mechanisms of criminal justice work. They must also experience that knowledge by doing the same activities they have observed if they want to do such work as graduates. By actively completing the mechanisms of the career they have chosen, they will understand why they must do what they do and understand how to create the outcomes they seek on the job.

The other process, dialogue, involves dialogue with self and with others. The student dialogues with self to reflect on what the student is learning and to try and place new information in a framework for usage. By thinking about newly acquired knowledge, the student is attempting to understand why this knowledge might be useful to the student and of what use the knowledge will be to the future of the student. The dialogue with others involves receiving the knowledge from the instructor and any discussion the instructor can create between the student and instructor, other students in the course, and even professionals and experts. Such dialogue creates an understanding of different perspectives on the topic, different experiences with the knowledge, and an appreciation of the various applications for the new knowledge.

Model of Active Learning (Adapted from Fink)

| Experience of: | Dialogue with: |
|---|---|
| Doing | Self |
| Observing | Others |

Using the model of active learning in the criminal justice classroom can be accomplished with a three prong approach. The first prong involves expanding usage of learning experiences created by the instructor. The instructor should go beyond the traditional lecture that creates the students' dialogue with self and others. The next step is to develop innovative applied learning activities that create the experiences of observing and doing. The purpose of this book is to suggest various applied learning activities that can be adapted and customized to the criminal justice classroom. These activities also may inspire additional innovative application strategies for the classroom.

The second prong of using the model, according to Fink, involves using the power of interaction. The higher order learning outcomes are created from the power created from the interaction of dialoging with self and others and also having the experiences of observing and doing the work of the criminal justice professional. The lecture is still an important part of the process, but learning will be enhanced with the addition of small group discussions (dialoguing with others), discussions with criminal justice professionals (dialoging with others), watching professionals perform their field work (observational experience), and actively engaging in activities that mirror the work of the professional (the experience of doing).

The third and final prong of using active learning in the classroom involves creating a dialectic between experience and dialogue. The processes of dialogue with self and others helps develop the meaning of the knowledge learned. It creates the beliefs and values in the student necessary to become

3

the criminal justice professional. They understand the meaning behind what they are expected to do as professionals which helps them become part of the criminal justice solution. The instructor should design courses to combine the experience and dialogue processes to create the learning necessary for lifelong application.

The purpose of this book is to also help instructors create the passion and motivation to become a criminal justice professional. The use of active and applied learning strategies also can develop the passion and motivation that creates not just the love of learning necessary to become a good professional, but the passion and motivation graduates will need to deal with the difficulties of criminal justice work and the desire to make a difference. These active, applied learning strategies can create the necessary student engagement to accomplish those goals.

*Student Engagement*

Motivation for learning and for the criminal justice career can be developed and enhanced through methods of student engagement. The activities described in this book accompanied by several other learning strategies create the appropriate student engagement necessary to create appropriate learning outcomes and to produce criminal justice graduates useful to the discipline.

Motivation in the classroom can be either extrinsic, which is learning to receive a reward (grade, prize, job), or intrinsic, which is learning for the sake of learning, acquiring knowledge for the love of it, the passion of doing the job. Implementing applied learning activities with methods designed to enhance the love of learning and to stoke the passion for criminal justice will create the long-term commitment necessary for students to successfully complete their degrees and to maintain long and fruitful careers in criminal justice.

The methods for student engagement involve first reducing the use of extrinsic rewards. Moving students away from the extrinsic reward structure of working for grades or getting the job may seem difficult, but the following methods are based on intrinsic motivation and can be easily implemented along with the applied learning activities.

4

Students in the traditional classroom sometimes complain of unclear and inconsistent expectations. Clarity and consistency of expectations reduces fear and apprehension and often allows students to more readily obtain the outcomes of instruction as designed by the instructor. When they know clearly what they should do to write a paper, to present a topic to the class, or to complete an exercise, they will do so enthusiastically and will reap the benefits of the experience.

The classroom environment can be developed to create better student engagement. This is accomplished by making students feel welcome and supported. Sometimes students are dialoguing with themselves about whether they will be a good criminal justice professional or about whether they can learn some of the more difficult material in criminal justice. Instructor dialogue with the students, as well as having criminal justice professionals assist with this process, can give students the mirror they need to see themselves in the criminal justice field. Such dialogues can help students understand that their instructors and even criminal justice professionals have struggled with complex knowledge and that the course is designed to help them overcome those complexities. Students begin to realize that they will not be judged for their mistakes, but will be given the chance to learn and to overcome the difficulties they may face with the material.

The classroom environment also is enhanced by responding positively to student questions and praising students for their good work. Students are sometimes afraid to ask questions for fear of being judged as inadequate by the instructor or for fear of being ridiculed by their peers. When all questions, whether they are good questions or not, are handled positively and respect is shown to the students, the dialogue between students and the instructor is increased and learning is enhanced. Knowing that you have given them praise also allows the students to feel you care about their learning which enhances their image of themselves as future criminal justice professionals.

The caring approach of the instructor is the key to the image building of students and their image of themselves as future criminal justice professionals. Developing quality relationships with students by actively engaging them in classroom activities, inspiring their desire to learn, and mentoring them as they develop their career aspirations will all assist in the process of bringing students through the process of becoming criminal justice professionals. Students who are at-risk or come from populations who do not typically seek criminal justice careers will likely be more successful. This process will help change the dynamics of those who do criminal justice work. When they feel connected to school and their instructor, they also will feel they are a part of the criminal justice discipline.

Student engagement also is enhanced by breaking larger tasks into smaller goals. Many of the course outcomes of criminal justice higher education involve higher order critical thinking skills and analytical abilities. Sometimes students fall short of these expectations. The students receive poor grades, and may even decide to quit the program. By using applied learning activities, many of these higher order learning outcomes can be broken into their component parts and students can incrementally achieve the higher order goals they may not have been previously prepared for. College students, for example, are expected to write good papers and use appropriate referencing processes and styles. Often, students have not received the training to do this, so the instructor becomes disappointed in the student which creates an uncomfortable environment and the self-image of the students may decline. Using incremental applied learning strategies that teach the student how to develop and write a good paper helps everyone accomplish their goals.

Students often believe that classroom failure is not an option. How instructors grade assignments may create those expectations. Instructors should be more concerned that students master the learning rather than whether they succeed or fail on an assignment. Mastery learning allows the student to work on an assignment until the outcome is achieved. Grades are based on effort as opposed to correctness. Instructors can enhance this process by evaluating work in a timely manner and giving clear and concise feedback to help the student in their next attempt. Students also should not be compared to each other, but to their commitment to learning. Students learn in different ways and on different timelines so working with those student differences and using applied learning strategies, will create more success for more students.

6

*Criminal Justice Students and Active Learning*

Criminal justice students can benefit greatly from instructors who use the model for active learning in their course designs. The knowledge, skills, and abilities that make up the course outcomes in criminal justice curriculums are highly suited to active learning strategies. The use of discussions permits the interaction necessary to obtain the understanding of the concepts, values, and missions of criminal justice.

The exercises that can be used to illustrate the activities of the criminal justice professional allow for the observation and application necessary to be able to function as a criminal justice graduate. Such exercises can make the entire criminal justice curriculum applicable to the student who may not be able to make the connection between textbook reading and actual work in the field.

Some of the criminal justice curriculum, such as research methods, often is frustrating for students because they find the course objectives confusing and difficult and then they do not see how they will use the knowledge as graduates. Instead of teaching students about research methods through the traditional lecture, having them actually do applied criminal justice research helps overcome the frustration, allows them to do well in the course, and also helps them understand how research is used in the field. The difference in teaching research methods with active learning strategies is overwhelming.

*Active, Applied Learning Activities Defined*

This book contains multiple suggestions of applied learning activities for the typical criminal justice curriculum. The reader will notice the range of activities is enormous, from the simple to the complex, from a general discussion to an activity that requires substantial time, space, and even equipment or supplies. An active, applied learning activity is any activity or exercise that creates the process of doing or discussing a topic to produce a course outcome. As suggested by Fink, the best activity is one that integrates discussion with self, discussion with others, observation of others doing the outcome, and finally the student taking part in the process by doing something.

Being creative is the key to developing an applied learning activity. Almost anything in the criminal justice curriculum can be translated into an applied activity that will create the learning necessary for the student to take the knowledge forward into their professional career. The key is to create the learning, connect it to the student in some manner, and have it in the mind of the graduate when they need it in their professional career. The act of doing creates that process.

### Customizing Applied Learning Activities for the Classroom

The activities provided in this book are simply suggestions for what could be done to teach outcomes in specific areas of criminal justice. It is important to remember that the criminal justice classroom varies greatly and can impact how exercises are conducted. Small classes can conduct exercises that may prove more difficult in a larger class. Some exercises will work better with graduate students rather than undergraduate students and vice versa. In addition, many criminal justice courses are taught online or through some other form of distance technology which means some exercises will have to be modified for those conditions.

Instructors should customize these exercises and any others that they create for the setting in which they will be used. The style of the instructor also will dictate some customization of the exercises. The instructor should feel free to make whatever changes are suitable to the setting, the type of students being taught, and the style of the instructor.

### Conducting Applied Learning Activities

Most instructors start out using the traditional lecture because it is the easiest method to use and the one most of us have experienced with our own instructors. The reason that the traditional lecture has remained a primary method of instruction is because it fits within our comfort zone and often keeps us from the unknown world of applied activities. To conduct an applied learning activity means taking a risk. You will worry about whether it will work. You also will worry that you might lose control of your students as you try to get them to take part in the process. Each of those concerns is valid. It is risky business.

The risk is worth the effort because of the learning that occurs from the process. Conducting an exercise for the first time will not be as comfortable as the tenth time you conduct it. The first time you do anything will not be as good as it will be with lots of practice. You have to start somewhere and believe it or not, students are very forgiving of the instructor who is attempting to make learning more useful and interesting to them. You also will learn how to modify, refine, and customize the exercise with feedback from your students. In addition, it is important to remember that an exercise that works well with one group of students may not work as well the next time with a different group of students. Again, use your own critical thinking skills to modify, refine, and customize until you find what works for your students.

This chapter has primarily discussed what the students will receive from your use of applied learning strategies. They will indeed learn more and will be able to use that learning as professionals. The use of applied learning also will enhance and develop your professional skills as an educator. Instructors often worry or are concerned about the results of student evaluations. Instructors express frustration that the student evaluations of instruction are unfair or not valid. Believe it or not, but the use of applied learning strategies can take your professional teaching skills to a new level. You will not have to wonder about the validity of the student evaluation of instruction ever again. Why? Because your students will be learning, they will be excited, they will even come to class more than ever before. They will be less likely to cheat or to complain about your instruction. Many of the typical teaching concerns are washed away with the use of the active learning model because teaching and learning are functioning at their best.

Use this book as a professional tool to enhance your teaching skills and to create the learning outcomes that will make your students the professionals needed in criminal justice. Take the risk if you have never tried such activities before. If you have been using applied activities in your courses, then use this book as a collection of new ideas to work from. Also, you may recognize exercises you have already used before. Pat yourself on the back for doing these exercises with your students whether you have already taken the risk or just plan to take the risk. It is worth the learning that happens for your students.

The activities are listed according to subject matter areas such as the Criminal Justice System, Criminology, Policing, Courts, Criminal Law, Corrections, Juvenile Justice, and Ethics. Some of the activities can be used in more than one subject matter area. The additional subject matter area(s) are identified within parentheses at the end of the particular activity. In addition, major course concepts will be highlighted in **bold** within the activity for ease in determining which activities might be chosen for the teaching of the subject matter area and teaching specific concepts.

## References

Bloom, B.S. (1984). *Taxonomy of educational objectives.* Boston, MA: Allyn and Bacon.

Brewster, C. and J. Fager (2000). *Increasing student engagement and motivation: From time-on-task to homework.* Retrieved February 7, 2007 from Northwest Regional Educational Laboratory Website: http://www.nwrel.org/request/oct00/textonly.html

Fink, L.D. (1999). *Model of active learning.* Retrieved February 7, 2007 from University of Oklahoma Instructional development Program Website: http://honolulu.hawaii.edu/intranet/committees/FacDevCom/guidebk/teachti p/active.htm.

# CHAPTER 2

# THE CRIMINAL JUSTICE SYSTEM

## Criminal Justice

1. **Interest in Criminal Justice:** Find out how many students in the class are not criminal justice majors, and ask them why they are taking the class. This exercise can lead to a discussion of the fact that criminal justice is an area of interest to almost everyone, not just those majoring in the field.

2. Invite members from your local criminal justice community to come to class and discuss their **jobs**, as well as **internships** their agencies might have available. (Careers)

3. Have a panel consisting of a police officer, a prosecuting attorney, and a defense attorney come to class to discuss their **roles in the criminal justice process** from initial contact through appeal/post conviction remedies.

4. Bring news clippings of crime cases to class, and have students discuss where these cases would appear in the "**wedding cake model**" of criminal justice.

5. Prior to a discussion of the **perspectives on criminal justice**, have students write down their own perspectives of criminal justice. This can lead to a discussion of which perspective presented in the text is shared by the majority of the class.

6. Develop a paper discussing the **development of criminal justice in America**.

7. Interview members of the local police force and criminal court on the issues of **ethics** discussed in your text. Develop a paper on ethics in law enforcement and criminal courts. (Ethics)

8. Seek permission from the local criminal court to **follow a court case** through the formal criminal justice system. Develop a paper based on this case study. (Punishment and Sentencing)

9. Prior to discussing the **crime definition** chapter, ask students to write down how they think crime is defined. Have them discuss

11

their answers, and then have them determine if their answers are more closely aligned with the consensus view of crime, or the conflict view of crime. (Criminology)

10. Send students to a computer lab on campus and assign them to access the most recent data available from the **UCR** and the **NCVS**. Have them share their findings with the class. (Criminology, Victimization)

11. Invite a local police officer to come to class and discuss how the local police department reports crime for the **UCR**. (Policing)

12. Invite a local law enforcement agent to come to class to discuss **crime trends** in your area. (Policing)

13. On the web, find the federal, state, county and municipal **crime statistics** for your jurisdiction. Do they all seem to agree? Write a summary evaluation of their adequacy. (Criminology)

14. **Interview a practitioner** who actually works in the criminal justice field and give a 10-minute class report about the interview. Include a table of the organization of the practitioner's agency, the practitioner's opinion about the system, their career advice, their day-to-day activities on the job, and their opinion of the job. (Careers)

15. Using the web, access ten **job descriptions** of people working in the criminal justice system. (Careers)

16. Over the course of the term, students should track the **media coverage of crime** and then present their research in relation to the actual **crime rate** for this period. Students should attempt to determine if the media sensationalized crime during the term of the course. (Criminology, Victimization)

17. Have the students watch a television show about the criminal justice process prior to a field trip to a courthouse. Then, students should discuss in class the difference between the **image of the criminal justice system** as portrayed in the media and the reality of the system. This can be used to highlight the **crime control and due process models**. (Courts)

18. In regard to public perceptions about the severity of various offenses, Americans do not share a consensus about all of the

behaviors that are defined under law as "crimes." Students can test their own perceptions about the **definition of crimes** and explore the moral and political issues underlying crime definitions by discussing whether the following actions should be crimes:

a.  Exchanging money for sex between two consenting adults
b.  Playing poker for money with friends
c.  Taking a candy bar from a store without paying for it
d.  An industrial company pouring pollution into a river
e.  Attempting suicide
f.  Public drunkenness
g.  An employee taking a ballpoint pen home from the office for personal use
h.  Calling someone an ethnically/racially derogatory name

The exercise works most effectively by listing the eight behaviors on the board and then asking the class to immediately vote on each one. The discussion can proceed after a rough vote tally has been recorded on the board for each behavior.

a.  Exchanging Money for Sex between Consenting Adults.

This is often used as an example of the quintessential "victimless crime" because consenting adults are determining their own behavior. In fact, if not for the exchange of money, this behavior is legal (or virtually never prosecuted). When pressed to justify the criminalization of this behavior, some students may initially say, in effect, "it is immoral." This raises the question of whether or not criminal law does or should reflect morality, and moreover, whose morality? Note that not all "immoral" behaviors are defined as crimes. For example, although lying is considered immoral, it is illegal only in specific contexts (e.g., perjury during sworn testimony, reporting income on tax forms, etc.). Other students may note that money-for-sex should be a crime, not because of moral concerns, but because of social harms or risks caused by such behavior. The most common examples are the risk of sexually transmitted diseases (e.g., AIDS) and the association between prostitution and other kinds of crimes, especially robbery and the use of illegal drugs. It is interesting to note that prostitution has been legal in Nevada, the Netherlands, and

13

other places in which governments attempt to limit social harms through government regulation rather than through criminalization.

If relatively few students vote to make prostitution a crime, as often happens in college classes, ask the students why it is defined as a crime even though there may be (judging from the class vote) a lack of public support for its criminalization. Ask the students why they have not contacted their legislators to ask that prostitution be legalized. The point of this discussion is to note that there is no significant political constituency favoring the legalization of prostitution. People who are ambivalent about the criminalization of prostitution view it as much less important than many other policy issues (e.g., the economy, health care, education, etc.). Politicians find it convenient to support the status quo (i.e., the criminalization of prostitution) because there are no political benefits to be gained from legalization (i.e., the policy has no constituency), but there would be a significant cost (i.e., alienating those who are adamantly opposed). Moreover, the criminalization of prostitution maintains laws that are useful for law enforcement officers when they wish to sweep the streets in specific neighborhoods in the course of combating drug trafficking, loitering, and other behaviors that annoy neighborhood residents.

b.  Playing Poker for Money with Friends.

This is another action that some may characterize as a "victimless crime." Students may ask, "What is the harm?" Counterarguments may focus on the lack of government regulation of such gambling which, unlike in the regulated casinos of Las Vegas and Atlantic City, may lead to cheating, victimization, and, potentially, violent conflict. Alternatively, perhaps the government should have a paternalistic responsibility to protect people from themselves, especially gambling addicts who may spend their families' resources on gambling rather than on food, shelter, and the necessities of life. In essence, what kinds of potential harms are sufficiently serious to merit criminalization of an activity?

14

c.   Taking a candy bar from a store without paying for it.

AND

g.   Taking a ballpoint pen from the office for personal use.

Typically, students will be unanimous is characterizing the candy bar/store situation as a criminal act but relatively few students will conceptualize the pen/office situation in the same manner. In fact, they are virtually identical situations of taking an object of modest value belonging to someone else for personal use without the owner's permission: i.e., theft. Student may try to distinguish the situations by saying that people take pens from the office inadvertently or that people return pens to their offices after using them at home. However, these purported distinctions change the factual situation as given. Other common rationalizations include the idea that (1) businesses expect employees to take pens or that (2) pens are of modest value. Effective counterarguments are (1) convenience stores expect to be robbed, but that does not make such robberies acceptable and (2) the aggregate value of a loss of employee pens to large corporations (e.g., tens of thousands of employees of General Motors) may represent a huge cost that is passed to customers in higher prices for products. Moreover, where does one draw the line on what is acceptable for employees to take? A box of envelopes? A typewriter? A computer?

These two examples subtly, but effectively, lead students to confront the question of "who is a criminal?" Thus many students, who have or would themselves take a pen from an employer's office, cannot conceive of themselves as having committed a criminal act (i.e., stealing). However, when passing judgment on something that other people do, such as taking an item from a store, it is relatively easy to label "those people" as criminals. The underlying point, of course, is that criminals are not the "bad people" in society; they are people who have violated a criminal law. Nearly every adult American is a "criminal" in the sense of having violated some criminal statute (i.e., driving after drinking, misstating income on tax forms, etc.). Because middle-class college students

15

tend to have an "us v. them - good v. bad" conception of stark distinctions between criminals and law-abiding citizens, the comparison of the two theft situations can provide a useful, thought-provoking example.

d.   Industrial company pouring pollution into a river.

Typically, a large proportion of students will agree that this activity should be a crime. In fact, experience indicates that this example and the ballpoint pen/store example (c, g) are the two items most likely to garner unanimous support for criminalization. Interestingly, because of the politics of criminal justice, the pollution example may be among the least likely to be criminalized and prosecuted. Many kinds of pollution cases are settled with modest civil financial penalties or payment of clean up costs. Even if criminal sanctions are available under existing statutes, it is relatively unusual to prosecute individual business executives who are responsible for such activities. Because business interests possess significant political power (i.e., lobbyists, campaign contributions, personal relationships among business and political elites, etc.), they are frequently better positioned than others in society to influence legislatures' definitions of crimes and punishments and to receive respectful treatment from elected officials, including prosecutors and judges.

e.   Attempting suicide.

What harm is caused by attempting suicide? One argument may be that someone jumping from a building could harm other people. Alternatively, there are tangible costs in public expenditures for police and medical personnel called to the scene and intangible costs to the families of people who attempt to commit suicide. Fundamentally, however, even if there are paternalistic (i.e., help people with mental problems) or other reasons (i.e., costs to society) for government to seek prevention of suicides, is it appropriate to stigmatize troubled people through criminalization of such actions rather than through civil commitment statutes? Because punishment is the defining characteristic of the criminal law, should we punish those we are attempting to find help?

f.  Public drunkenness.

The challenge for students with this example is to think of any harm caused by public drunkenness that is not already covered by other criminal statutes. Assault and property damage, for example, are already covered. If students seek to protect drunken people from harming themselves, then, as in the example concerning attempting suicide, the same issues exist concerning stigmatization and the application of punishment as a means to help troubled people. Because it is difficult to identify concrete social harms not already covered by other laws, the public drunkenness example is useful for illustrating the existence of laws that give police broad discretion to maintain order and to protect the sensibilities of society's dominant social classes. Who is likely to be arrested for public drunkenness, a homeless person lying by the doorway to an expensive restaurant or a man in a tuxedo stumbling out of the same restaurant?

h.  Calling someone an ethnically/racially derogatory name.

Although Americans' conceptions of freedom of speech tend to make relatively few students favor criminalization of ethnic/racial name-calling, it is interesting to note such activities may arguably cause the same potential harms that students may have used to justify criminalization in other examples. For example, such actions, like public drunkenness, may lead to assault or property damage. However, dominant political values, such as freedom of speech, may lead many Americans to discount the same potential harms that seemed threatening in other hypothetical contexts.

19. Have the students interview family members and friends, whose identities will be kept anonymous, about their experiences as **victims** of criminal activity. After each student presents his or her research, the class should then debate whether the experiences qualify as criminal offenses. This should illustrate the problems associated with measuring crime. (Victimization)

20. Debate whether the **War on Drugs** contributes to the **racism** in society. Is the criminal justice system racist? How? (Drugs)

21. Exercise: **System Attributes**

    Imagine that you are a county prosecutor. Briefly describe how the attributes of the criminal justice system (discretion, resource dependence, sequential tasks, and filtering) would affect your relationships, decisions, and actions with respect to each of the following. (Courts)

    a. Police
    b. Defense Attorneys
    c. Trial Judges
    d. News Media

22. Describe, compare and contrast **the due process and crime control models of criminal justice**. Be sure to provide examples.

    Some main points: The due process model is primarily concerned with rights of defendants, creates an obstacle course to get a conviction and tends to be favored by liberals. The crime control model stresses repression of crime, efficiency in the criminal justice system, and harsh sentences to deter criminals.

23. Exercise: **The System**

    As part of an honors program at your college, the chairman of the Social Science Division has nominated you to represent the Criminal Justice Department in a 20th Century time capsule project. She is asking all departments to contribute material, to be placed in a sealed, weather proof container, which will be buried on the campus grounds. The capsule will be opened on 1/1/2101.

    She asks you to include at least ten simulated, representative documents or artifacts which reflect your study of the American Criminal Justice System and policing for the years 1900 to the present. What would you include? What would you include if she had asked you to reflect policing in the 19th century? 18th century?

24. **Discretion** allows the various "**gatekeepers**" at each stage of the criminal justice system the power to determine who continues and who is diverted from the system. Ask students to identify these gatekeepers and discuss their decision making process. That is, what are the factors that impact their choice to move a case further in the system?

18

# CHAPTER 3

# CRIMINOLOGY AND RESEARCH METHODS

## Criminology

1. Ask students to write down how they think crime is defined. Have them discuss their answers, and then have them determine if their answers are more closely aligned with the **consensus view of crime**, or the **conflict view of crime**. (Criminal Justice)

2. Send students to a computer lab on campus and assign them to access the most recent data available from the **UCR** and the **NCVS**. Have them share their findings with the class. (Criminal Justice, Victimization)

3. Have students discuss which **theories** they think offer the strongest explanations for crime. Encourage them to think of particular crimes that might not be explained by particular theories.

4. Receive permission from the county jail to conduct interviews with persons who might be labeled **career criminals**. Develop a paper based on these interviews. Be sure to include a theory component.

5. Talk to a sociologist at your school and discuss **strain theories** of crime. Where does all this theorizing begin? How do sociologists view crime?

6. Who or what agency in your community **diagnoses criminals**? Does this agency have a website? Can you describe what the agency or individual does?

7. On the web, find the federal, state, county and municipal **crime statistics** for your jurisdiction. Do they all seem to agree? Write a summary evaluation of their adequacy. (Criminal Justice)

8. Assuming that our legal system is **neo-classical**, it sees behavior as chosen activity yet it also excuses some behavior under some circumstances such as **justification defenses** and **excuse defenses**. Please give your view on this question: "Have we struck a good balance between what we hold persons responsible for and what

we excuse?" Please write your opinion in a 1,500 word essay and cite the sources for all data used.

9. Over the course of the term, students should track the **media coverage of crime** and then present their research in relation to the actual crime rate for this period. Students should attempt to determine if the media sensationalized crime during the term of the course. (Criminal Justice, Victimization)

10. Exercise: **Theories about the Causes of Crime**

On his way home from school, a fourteen-year-old boy from a poor family stops at a convenience store. When he thinks the clerk is not looking, he puts a bottle of orange juice under his coat and heads for the door. The clerk catches him and calls the police. How might one explain the boy's criminal action according to each of the following theories about causes of crime?

    a. Biological Explanations
    b. Psychological Explanations
    c. Social Structure Theory
    d. Social Process Theory

11. Select a recent crime from a local newspaper. Ask students to identify how three different criminologists working from either the **consensus view of crime, conflict view of crime,** or **interactionist view of crime** might go about explaining the occurrence of that particular criminal incident and society's response to it.

12. **Gun Control** is a hot topic in the United States. Poll the class as to their views on gun control. Divide the class into two groups. One group will be pro gun control and the second group will be anti-gun control. Have each group prepare a presentation for their side. Poll the class again to see if the results changed after the presentations.

13. Break students into groups and have them construct a short self-report survey on **underage drinking** at their school. What questions should be included? How easy or difficult is it to construct a proper survey? How might they sample their fellow students? How might different sampling procedures lead to different results? What problems may arise like, for example,

memory problems, lying, and revelations of illegal behaviors? (Research Methods)

14. Have the students examine the differences between **females** and males in their levels of criminal involvement. Find, or develop, a list of about 50 delinquent acts including alcohol and drug use, minor criminal acts, and more serious criminal acts. Hand this form out to the students. They are to mark on the form whether they are female or male and each item they committed prior to the age of 18. Have them turn these forms in and then redistribute them to the class. On the board, write two sets of 1-50 (one for male sheets and one for female sheets). Have the students place on the board a check mark next to the items that are marked on their sheet. Taking into account the gender distribution within your class, discuss those items where females and males report similar levels of offending and those items where there is a clear disparity. (Women)

15. There are four main **victimization theories** as to why individuals are victimized. Divide the class into four groups and have each discuss one of the theories: **victim precipitation theory, lifestyle theory, deviant place theory, and routine activities theory**. Have each group explain the theory to the class and cite examples of known cases. (Victimization)

16. Not every person in the United States is at equal risk of **victimization**. Using National Crime Victimization Survey information, have students develop a composite for that individual at highest risk and that individual at lowest risk. (Research Methods)

17. Discuss recent films such as *Natural Born Killers, Hannibal,* and *Blow*. Were these criminals **rational**? Did they make a **choice** to be a criminal or were there other contributing elements to their criminality? Could any of these individuals have avoided criminal behaviors or was it beyond their control?

18. Provide students with information on the "hot spots" of crime on your campus. Then, break them into groups and ask the students to apply concepts from **situational crime prevention** and **defensible space** in an effort to reduce criminal incidents in these areas.

19. Although most Americans support the death penalty, there remains an ongoing debate as to its effectiveness as a **deterrent** against murder. Divide the class into two groups. Have one group develop a presentation in support of the deterrent effect of capital punishment and the other group against the deterrent effect. Students, then, can discuss which position is the stronger of the two. (Punishment and Sentencing)

20. Can **personality traits** predispose an individual to commit crimes? Divide the class into groups. One group is to describe a successful individual. Another group is to describe a not so successful individual. A third group is to describe a criminal. Are there distinct traits for the successful individual, the not so successful individual, and the criminal individual?

21. Many states provide pictures on the Internet of those criminals who are registered as a sex offender. Select four such pictures making sure that three of them fit **Lombroso's "born criminal"** and **Sheldon's "mesomorph" typologies**. The fourth picture should look like your traditional college-aged student. Then, have the students decide who is and is not a sex offender among the group. Discussions can center on the usefulness of physical characteristics in identifying criminals and the stereotypes that are predominate within our society concerning offender types.

22. A variety of **mental disorders** have been linked to criminal activities. Have students discuss whether those criminals who have been deemed mentally ill should be incarcerated for their offenses or be housed in a mental health facility. Is it appropriate to incarcerate someone with a mental illness? Are they "getting away" with the crime if they are housed in a mental health facility instead of a prison? (Criminal Law)

23. Have the students examine the Los Angeles Riot of April 29, 1992. Which components of **Strain Theory** are evident in this devastating event? Would other theories such **as Differential Opportunity** be relevant to this riot?

24. **Strain Theory** proposes that lower-class citizens turn to crime, in part, as a result of frustrations they face when attempting to achieve socially approved goals. Have students investigate the various agencies and programs in your community that are

oriented towards providing assistance to this group of citizens. Students should pay close attention to barriers that may interfere with the agency's ability to provide services to all in need (for example, limited resources, limited space, regulations concerning substance use, and financial need requirements).

25. **Cohen** provides an explanation for the development of **deviant subcultures** among young, lower-class males who are unable to "measure up" to the **middle-class measuring rods**. Ask students to reflect upon the various subcultures they saw within their high school. How might these vary according to how urban or rural the community was, the economic status of the students, the gender ratio within the school, and whether the school was public or private?

26. Examine the career and life of Robert Downey, Jr. Downey, a renowned actor, has a serious addiction to drugs. Has Downey been labeled as an addict or a criminal? Has **labeling theory** been a factor in the treatment of Downey? What elements of **social process theory** apply to the Downey situation? (Drugs)

27. Hirschi proposes that the stronger the **social bond** to society, the less likely one is to offend. Ask students to investigate what agencies and programs are available in their community to strengthen each of the four elements of the social bond. The following provides examples: attachment - Big Brothers/Big Sisters, commitment - banks that advertise special savings accounts for children, involvement - midnight basketball, and belief - youth leaders who are members of community boards.

28. The following is a quick exercise to demonstrate the power of a **label**. Ask students to close their eyes and visualize a police officer (you may have to ask them to humor you here). Then, one-by-one, tell them the police officer is a female, Hispanic, 47 years of age, and a lesbian. The point is not how common this combination of characteristics exists, but rather how drastically their perception changes once a new "label" is revealed. (Race)

29. Divide the class into three groups. Have each group review one of the **Conflict theorists**: Bonger, Dahrendorf, or Vold. Compare and contrast the theorists, the culture in which they lived, the economic times, and the relevance of their theory in today's pop culture.

30. Taking a recent case of a female offender that was featured in the local newspaper, ask students to explain her offense as a **radical feminist** would. That is, examine the extent to which the offender may have been disadvantaged by a patriarchal society in her various educational, economic, and social endeavors. Was her crime a reflection of her less valued position in society? Is there any mention of her being a crime victim in the past?

31. The **peacemaking** movement advocates for more "humanist solutions to crime." Break students into groups and have them brainstorm as to what these humanist solutions might look like. Remember that Pepinsky and Quinney advocate for mediation and conflict resolution policies. (Ethics)

32. Conduct an anonymous survey of student's deviant behavior as adolescents. Have the class analyze results and discuss delinquent behavior in terms of the **developmental theories**.

33. Find an article in the local newspaper featuring a crime committed by a very young offender. Explain the case to the students and have them develop a timeline for this person's life according to **life course theories**. That is, what might we expect from someone who has started a criminal career so early in life? What would be necessary for this person to age out of offending in the future?

34. Assign groups to various **terrorism** events that have occurred in the last 10 years in the United States and abroad. Key events may include the September 11, 2001 attack on the United States, the Oklahoma City Bombing, events in the Middle East, and the Unabomber. How have these events changed the United States? (Terrorism and Homeland Security)

35. **Workplace violence** costs American businesses billions of dollars each year. In addition to the most dangerous occupations such as being a police officer, correctional officer, or taxicab driver, have the students discuss violence they may have witnessed in the jobs they have held.

36. The website http://www.tolerance.org provides a map of **hate groups** for the nation and by state. Print off the map for your state and bring it to class for discussion. Are students even aware of the

number and range of recognized hate groups in their state? How active are these groups?

37. Have the class research current statistics for petty property crimes and **white-collar property crimes**. Discuss the results. What are the similarities? What are the differences?

38. **Credit card abuse** has become a billion dollar industry in the United States. Ask the students how many credit and debit cards they have in their name. Discuss their use in both secure and nonsecure sites on the Internet, over the telephone, and in various stores. How easy would it be for someone to gain access to their account? (Forensics and Technology)

39. Although the victim of a confidence game may lose large amounts of money, to what extent can we hold them partially responsible? Are they truly innocent victims of the con man or woman, or are they partly to blame because they participated in the get-rich-quick scheme? If we do hold the victim partly responsible, does this reduce the amount of **culpability** we place on the offender? (Victimization)

40. Have the class review various groups of **organized crime**. Discuss the different characteristics of the groups, their areas of operation, and their specific crime specializations.

41. **White-collar crimes** are crimes that are committed because of access within a business structure. While few students will have held white-collar positions, they will have had experience in blue- and pink-collar jobs. Discuss the various forms of crime they or other coworkers were able to commit because of the jobs they held.

42. The vast majority of persons with a computer connected to the Internet and e-mail have had experience with some form of a **computer virus**. Discuss those activities that place our personal computers at highest risk. What can we do to better protect our computer system? Allow the students to discuss how their computer got "infected." (Forensics and Technology)

43. Look at the statutes concerning various **drugs**. Have the class debate the issue of legalizing any or all types of drugs. Are the penalties currently in place appropriate? Why or why not? (Drugs)

44. Divide the class into two sections. Have one argue in favor of **decriminalizing prostitution** and the other argue against decriminalization. Obviously, key points in favor of decriminalization will include the ability to monitor the health status of the prostitutes, to generate tax dollars for the community, and to provide a safer working environment for the prostitutes. Key points against decriminalization will include the possibility of youth being exposed to information on sexuality at a younger age, a disconnection between sex and love, and a general acceptance of sexual promiscuity in society.

45. Although we have witnessed a decrease in the rates of many crimes in recent years, currently we are at an all-time high in the number of people under some form of **correctional supervision**. Have students discuss how this can be so. One obvious answer is that we have a wider variety of supervision options available to us today than in the past. (Community Corrections and Probation)

46. Assign each student a county in your state to profile on the basis of **social, economic, and criminological factors**. For the social picture the students may want to include such items as population size, rural versus urban area, rate of college graduates, divorce rate, etc. For the economic picture the students may want to include such items as percentage below poverty, average family income, percentage unemployed, rate of home ownership, etc. Census data are useful for the social and economic variables. Criminological factors, such as crime rates, arrest rates, number of officers, etc., can be obtained from your state crime information center. The focus of the written assignment, then, is to tie the various social and economic forces operating within the county to the levels and types of crimes identified.

47. Ask students to select a recent crime from a local newspaper. They can spend a short amount of time laying out the facts of the case or merely have them attach the article to their final paper. Then, they are to define and **apply one theory** that does a good job explaining this type of offense and one theory that does a bad job explaining this type of offense. They are to integrate facts from the article to support their argument. This paper works best if the student applies a specific theory, like Routine Activities Theory, rather than a more "umbrella" theory, like Social Disorganization Theories.

48. Assign each student a **theory** for which they are to identify local, state, and national programs, policies, or laws that support its premise. A discussion of the theory, its policy implications, and its applications provide for the three parts to the paper.

49. Have each student select one type of crime. They should provide the legal definition for the offense, incidence rates at both the state and national levels, and clearance rates at both the state and national levels. To what extent does this crime in your state reflect **nationwide trends**? (Criminal Law)

50. **Street crimes (violent and property), enterprise crimes, and public order crimes** vary in definition, incidence level, and how society views them. Either have students compare and contrast across these three large crime classifications or have them select one crime from each of the three categories to use as a representative of that group of offenses. Students can then discuss how not all crimes are alike or viewed as such.

51. Have your students look up the case of John Hinckley shooting President Ronald Reagan. Explore his motives and rationalizations and try to determine if this was the act of **a sane man** or an assassin. (Criminal Law)

52. If there is any validity to **the biological theories** that crime is something an individual cannot control because he is biologically pre-disposed to commit crime, then discuss the purpose of punishment in the American criminal justice system.

53. Have a local member of your police department speak to your class about **routine activity theory** and its application to community policing. (Policing)

54. If possible, arrange a tour of the **socially disorganized** section of your town. Analyze the amount of graffiti and disorganization in that neighborhood.

55. Invite a city councilman to your class to discuss what steps are being taken to improve the **worst neighborhoods** in your city.

56. Examine the **crime statistics** for your town from your local police department. What areas of your city have the most and the least crime?

## Victimization

1. Send students to a computer lab on campus and assign them to access the most recent data available from the **UCR** and the **NCVS**. Have them share their findings with the class. (Criminology, Criminal Justice)

2. Write a research paper on the impact of **gangs** on crime and **victimization trends**. (Gangs)

3. Interview a victim who has made an **impact statement**. What is the victim's opinion of the process?

4. Over the course of the term, students should track the **media** coverage of crime and then present their research in relation to the actual crime rate for this period. Students should attempt to determine if the media sensationalized crime during the term of the course. (Criminology, Criminal Justice)

5. Have the students interview family members and friends, whose identities will be kept anonymous, about their experiences as victims of criminal activity. After each student presents his or her research, the class should then debate whether the experiences qualify as criminal offenses. This should illustrate the problems associated with **measuring crime**. (Criminal Justice)

6. Ask the students to develop an interview instrument to be used by police officers in interviewing victims of **domestic violence**.

   What questions should be asked and what information should be conveyed in the course of the police officer's interaction with a victim? In examining the questions developed by the students, attention should be paid to the role implications and objectives of particular questions selected for use. Do the questions (and information to be conveyed to the victim) reflect a service orientation or a law enforcement orientation? Are there special issues of sensitivity that will require questions to be asked in a certain way? What does this exercise show about the difficulties involved in encounters between the police and citizens? (Policing, Criminal Investigation)

7. In what ways might a person **become a victim** and need assistance from the police? Students might suggest that a person could become a victim of burglary, robbery, assault, rape, theft, etc.

8. Do you feel the media are sometimes insensitive to victims and could also be part of the **second injury of victimization**? If so, can you give examples? Examples might be interviews with victims, photos of assault victims, or bodies of murdered persons.

9. Should victims play a larger role in the criminal justice system? To what extent should victims play a role in the **prosecution and punishment** of their assailants? (Punishment and Sentencing)

   Possible discussion points: **Victim impact statements**, victim's wishes in sentencing, mandatory victim testimony, victims advocates as part of the courtroom work group.

10. What inroads has the **victims' rights movement** made regarding changes in the criminal justice system and process?

    Possible discussion points: Victim/witness assistance programs, victim compensation programs, victims' bills of rights, victim impact statements, Victims' Rights Amendment.

11. As the U.S. Constitution sets out **rights** for the accused, should victims gain benefits and rights at the expense of defendants' rights?

    Possible discussion point. Consider the defendants' rights. Are there any implicit rights guaranteed to victims by the U.S. Constitution? Should courts give the victims a larger role, or can a compromise be reached?

12. What negative drawbacks could increased **victims' rights** have on the criminal justice process?

    Possible discussion points: Increased trial delays, increased workload, harsher sentences, increased costs, increased litigation and appeals, increased victim frustration.

13. Consult your **states' rules or code of criminal procedure** on plea bargaining and the entry of guilty pleas. Do these rules provide any enough protection for defendants and any for crime victims? (Criminal Law)

14. Have students visit the portion of the website of the American Bar Association (ABA) that lists ABA standards for the prosecution of cases.

    http://www.abanet.org/crimjust/standards/pfunc_toc.html

    After they have reviewed these standards, ask them to respond in written form to the following questions: (Criminal Investigation, Courts)

    a.  What are the **ABA standards** for an **extrajudicial statement**?

    b.  Is a prosecutor's office expected to offer legal advice to a law enforcement agency concerning criminal matters?

    c.  What is the ABA standard for relationships with victims and witnesses by the prosecutor?

15. There are four main **victimization theories** as to why individuals are victimized. Divide the class into four groups and have each discuss one of the theories: **victim precipitation theory, lifestyle theory, deviant place theory, and routine activities theory**. Have each group explain the theory to the class and cite examples of known cases. (Criminology)

16. Although most jurisdictions allow for **victim/witness impact statements** to be offered at the sentencing phase, much debate continues to surround this practice. Have students identify the pros and cons for the victim, offender, and criminal justice system as a whole.

17. Although the victim of a confidence game may lose large amounts of money, to what extent can we hold them partially responsible? Are they truly innocent victims of the con man or woman, or are they partly to blame because they participated in the get-rich-quick scheme? If we do hold the victim partly responsible, does this reduce the amount of **culpability** we place on the offender? (Criminology)

18. There are thousands of agencies with the mission of providing **services to victims of crime**. Have your students complete an in-depth investigation into a specific agency at the local, state, or national level. The paper should include an historical look at the agency, provide statistics on the number and type of victims they

assist, offer descriptions of the services provided, give an explanation of the philosophy of the agency, discuss funding sources, and provide information on the location of the agency. You may even want to include a personal interview with a representative of the agency.

## Research Methods

1. Discuss the **importance of research in criminal justice**. Research is important in the criminal justice field because it can determine which strategies, interventions and experiments are effective or ineffective in preventing and reducing crime and disorder and providing service to the community.

2. Have students design and conduct **a survey** (campus, neighborhood or law enforcement agency). Surveys can be conducted on a wide range of topics including fear of crime, crime reporting, police attitudes, community attitudes, victimization surveys, etc.

   Some ready-made surveys may be available from the Office of Community Oriented Policing Services and other community policing or crime prevention websites.

3. Ask students to write down reasons why they may have not done as well in a particular course as they would have liked. Collect those reasons and use them as illustrations of **errors in human inquiry**. By reading them aloud to the class, ask students to classify them as either a legitimate reason or an error. If it is an error, have them identify which one.

4. Bring in examples of various **research questions** that deal with crime, criminals, criminal law, or criminal justice policy. Ask students to comment on which **purpose of research** each example illustrates. Next, have students suggest research questions about dorm life, campus life, or any topic of their choice, and ask them to identify a purpose for each suggestion.

5. Bring a journal article to class for students to read. Break students down into groups and have them answer the following questions:

   a. What is **the theory** used in the article?

b. Identify the **variables** used in the article.

c. Does the article test a **hypothesis**? If so, explain it.

d. Is the research applied in nature?

Have each group select a spokesperson and then compare answers between groups.

6. Show a video in class from the History Channel or Arts & Entertainment dealing with crime and criminals. (There are great series on both of these networks that would be instructive and most videos are less than $30.) Discuss with students after viewing the piece the following:

a. What could explain the behavior exhibited in the video?

b. Have them identify a **theory and/or paradigm** that may explain what they saw.

c. Have students develop a **hypothesis** based upon the video that could be tested.

d. Could their hypothesis be used in applied research?

e. Ask students to identify **policy implications**.

7. Using your campus as a framework, come up with as many examples of potential projects as you can which use each of the following **units of analysis**.

a. Individuals

b. Groups

c. Organizations

d. Social Artifacts

8. Research indicates that there is a relationship between inmate visits from family and friends and the likelihood of recidivism upon release. Have students suggest an example of a **research design** that uses the relationship between visits and recidivism for each of the following:

a. Cross-sectional study

b. Longitudinal study
   - Trend study
   - Cohort study
   - Panel study

9. Bring to class a summary of **Marvin Wolfgang's Philadelphia study**. Discuss the technique used and the results. Ask students to suggest an alternative manner of completing such a project using something other than a **cohort design**. Discuss the challenges of doing similar research today.

10. Bring a journal article featuring an **experimental design** to class for students to read. Have students answer the following questions:

    a. What technique was used to select subjects and assign them to groups?

    b. What are the independent and dependent variables?

    c. What threats exist in this design?

    d. What conclusions can be made from this research?

    e. What suggestions can be offered to address the threats to the study?

11. Show the video *Quiet Rage* detailing the **Stanford Prison Simulation**. Let the students identify the manner in which participants were selected, the independent and dependent variables, the threats to validity of the study and how the researchers handled (or didn't handle) those threats.

12. Have students bring to class examples of research using the following techniques...

    a. any **probability sampling** method
    b. any **non-probability sampling** method

    Have students present a summary of their research examples to the class focusing upon the sampling method and the data gathering method.

13. Using the *Sourcebook of Criminal Justice Statistics* illustrate by using different charts, tables, etc. the **various ways researchers gather data.** Include some UCR data, some NCVS data and some attitudinal findings. Ask students to comment on the advantages and disadvantages of each technique. Ask students to suggest alternative methods of gathering similar data and what the advantages and disadvantages of these may be.

14. Propose a topic to your students and have them write a series of questions that represent **open-ended, closed-ended, matrix and contingency questions**.

15. Write several questions on the board that illustrate **ambiguous or negative items** and ask the students to recognize the problem in each and to offer solutions to the problems.

16. Propose a class project where students will break down into groups and conduct a **small-scale field research project** on campus. After the students have been assigned groups have them decide upon a project, identify how they will record data and use one class meeting for them to collect data. For the next class meeting have the students report their findings along with any problems that they encountered.

    Suggestions for projects:

    a.  Collect data from the cafeteria on seating arrangements by race or gender.

    b.  Collect data from elevators on campus identifying how people stand (either facing the door or with back turned toward the door) or whether conversations continue.

17. Bring several newspaper editorials to class that deal with some topic of crime/criminals or laws. Make copies of the editorials for the students. Have students identify how they would classify and complete a **content analysis** on the editorials.

18. **Program evaluation**: Identify in class a local criminal justice agency that has a program that has received negative media attention. Ask students to identify what they believe to be the goals of the agency, the outcomes of the agency and how they would evaluate the agency if asked to do so. Next, ask the students, in light of the media criticism, if they believe the agency has been accurately represented. Does the criticism reflect the goals? Personnel? Or something else.

19. Start with several data sets to illustrate for the class the **measures of central tendency** and **measures of dispersion**.

    a.  Have one data set be very compact with little variation in range.

b. Select another data set that illustrates dispersion with a great deal of variation.

c. As a class for each data set compute the:
   - Mode
   - Median
   - Mean
   - Range
   - Standard Deviation

d. End with a discussion about the inferences that can be made about a set of data by looking at the measures of central tendency and dispersion.

20. Break students into groups and have them construct a short **self-report survey** on underage drinking at their school. What questions should be included? How easy or difficult is it to construct a proper survey? How might they sample their fellow students? How might different sampling procedures lead to different results? What problems may arise like, for example, memory problems, lying, and revelations of illegal behaviors? (Criminology)

21. Not every person in the United States is at equal risk of victimization. Using **National Crime Victimization Survey** information, have students develop a **composite** for that individual at highest risk and that individual at lowest risk. (Criminology)

22. Exercise: **Analysis of a Research Article**

Have students obtain a research article from the criminal justice field and complete a critical analysis of the article. They must:

a. Identify the research question or problem statement.
b. Describe the methodology of the study.
c. Identify the respondents and the sampling plan.
d. Describe the quality of the literature review.
e. Describe the data collected.
f. Describe the findings and conclusion.
g. Evaluate the quality of the research based on the previous parts of the analysis.

23. Exercise: **How to Write a Literature Review**

Have students develop a criminal justice research question and gather literature to support the research question. Instruct them to read the literature and take notes about each aspect of each piece of literature using the article analysis format. Instruct the students to construct an outline of the major issues from the literature. The outline should be constructed to develop an argument of support for conducting a study to answer the research question. The student should then be instructed to flesh out the outline using the notes from their literature analysis. They should be instructed how to cite the literature as well. Once they have completed the fleshed out outline then they should be instructed how to transition the outline into a finished literature review.

24. Exercise: **Conducting a Research Interview**

Have students develop a structured and/or semi-structured interview protocol. Then have the students actually interview someone with the protocol. They should be taught to debrief their interview and how to write up their interview. They should then write a paper based on their interview results.

25. Exercise: **Creating a Scale**

Construct a scale in class with your students. Pick a scale topic such as deviance or motivation or any topic of your choice. Have the students develop scale items that measure the scale topic. Create 7-10 valid items and write them on the board. Use a 5-point Likert scale ranging from 1-5, strongly disagree to strongly agree. Help students create the most valid scale items possible and help them to write the questions to fit the Likert scaling. Then have the students answer the scale items and add up their own individual scores. Send around a blank sheet of paper and have students record their score anonymously. Create a histogram on the board and record their scores. Show them what their scores mean and interpret the histogram.

26. Exercise: **Creating Research Designs**

Have students develop multiple research designs for several criminal justice/criminology research questions. This exercise will teach them about using different types of research designs. Give them the research questions and have them either discuss possible designs in class or have them work in groups to develop the designs and report them back to class. Also, take one research question and have them develop multiple research designs for the same research question to demonstrate the multiple methods that can be used to study the same question.

27. Exercise: **Human Subjects Education**

    Teach students about the protection of human subjects in the research process by having them take an online tutorial on human subject's protection. They can even earn a certificate of completion by going to this website...

    http://cme.cancer.gov/clinicaltrials/learning/humanparticipant-protections.asp

28. Read about the **Zimbardo experiment** and have a group discussion as to what conclusions one can draw from it about the influence of an incarcerative setting. (Ethics)

# CHAPTER 4

# POLICING AND LAW ENFORCEMENT

## Policing

1. Invite a local police officer to come to class and discuss how the local police department reports crime for the **UCR**. (Criminal Justice)

2. Invite a local law enforcement agent to come to class to discuss **crime trends** in your area. (Criminal Justice)

3. During the 19th century, police departments often provided social services, such as emptying public privies and removing garbage. Engage students in a discussion of the types of **social services** police engage in today.

4. Invite a "seasoned" police officer to class (one who has been on the force at least since the 1960s) and ask him to discuss how the **role of policing** has changed over the years.

5. Invite **local representatives** of the various law enforcement agencies discussed in the text to come to class and discuss their jobs. (Careers)

6. If your local police department uses **crime mapping**, invite an officer to come to class and explain its usefulness for the department. (Criminal Investigation)

7. Invite a local police officer to come to class and discuss the **structure and organization** of the local police department.

8. See if you can arrange for students to go on police "**ride-alongs**."

9. If your campus is located in, or near, a large city, you could invite an **undercover agent** (or a former undercover agent) to come to class to discuss the realities of this type of work.

10. Divide students into small groups and have them develop **"community policing" models**.

11. Find out if any local agencies use **Civilian Review Boards**. If so, have the students interview board members and develop a paper on the topic.

12. Write a research paper on the development of **community policing**.

13. Divide the class into small groups. Have each group develop a list of qualifications for the **"ideal" police officer**. (Careers)

14. Invite police officers from several surrounding agencies to come to class and discuss the **qualifications** required by their departments, as well as **salaries** and **advancement** possibilities (e.g., how long does it take the average person to become a detective in each department?). (Careers)

15. Invite some **female police officers** to come to class and frankly discuss the issues they face as women in a traditionally male-oriented profession. (Careers)

16. Many police departments require that recruits be of "good moral character." This means that, to some extent, police officers are held to a **higher moral standard** than the average citizen. Encourage student discussion of this issue. (Ethics)

17. Invite both a judge and a police officer to come to class to discuss the impact of the **exclusionary rule** on policing. (Criminal Law)

18. Some larger cities have at least one **psychologist** who specializes in working with police officers. If one is located in your city, invite him or her to come to class to generally discuss the kinds of **problems faced by police**.

19. Have students interview local police officers about **the police culture** and then develop a paper on the topic.

20. Develop a research paper on **women in policing**. (Careers)

21. Write a paper on the impact of **corruption** on the area of policing. (Ethics)

22. Find the **police training manual** from the local police department and ask for an explanation of it from a police officer.

23. Find the website for the **community relations officers** in your area. Is **community policing** adequately explained?

24. Locate, distribute, and discuss the **ethics statement** of the local police or the sheriff. (Ethics)

25. Discuss the chapter material with a **juvenile officer** in the local police department. Does the interviewee accept the system as it is? Are there suggestions for improvement? What are the problems? (Juvenile Justice)

26. Visit the spokesman for the local **drug unit** from the police department. Discuss his or her views of the drug problem and compare them to your views. (Drugs)

27. On one hand, we value local autonomy and accountability of our law enforcers – especially the sheriff whom we elect, but on the other hand all the rest of our law enforcers are appointed by other politicians who shield the enforcers from the public. This raises the question: How much **accountability** can we expect from our law enforcers and how do we insure we get such accountability? Please justify your opinion in a 1,500 word essay and cite the sources for all data used. (Ethics)

28. In fighting crime, we have developed several **innovative police strategies** as well as continued to use traditional strategies. Based on the types of patrol, community policing, problem-solving policing, and other types of policing, give your opinion on which strategy or combination of strategies is most appropriate for the community in which your college is located. Please justify your opinion in a 1,500 word essay using data and cite the sources for all data.

29. Exercise: **The Fourth Amendment and the Exclusionary Rule**

A woman called the police to her home after her daughter was severely beaten earlier in the day by the daughter's boyfriend. The daughter agreed to use her key to let the officers into the apartment where the man was sleeping. The officers did not seek to obtain either an arrest warrant or a search warrant. After the daughter unlocked the apartment door, the officers entered and found a white substance, which later proved to be cocaine, sitting on a table. They arrested the sleeping man and charged him with narcotics offenses. The defendant sought to have the drugs excluded from evidence because the officers' warrantless search was based on permission from the girlfriend who had moved out of the apartment several weeks earlier and therefore had no authority to give the officers permission to enter and search. (Courts, Criminal Law)

a.   As the prosecutor, think about possible exceptions to the exclusionary rule, such as those discussed for the Fourth and Fifth Amendments, to make arguments about why the evidence should not be excluded.

b.   Now, imagine that you are the judge. Decide whether the evidence obtained in the warrantless search should be excluded. Provide reasons for your decision. Consider the words of the Fourth Amendment, the purposes of the Amendment, and the potential effects on society from the rule you formulate for this case.

30. Exercise: **The Fifth and Sixth Amendments**

After arresting a suspect for burglary, police officers learned that the suspect's nickname was "Butch." A confidential informant had previously told them that someone named "Butch" was guilty of an unsolved murder in another city. The police in the other city were informed about this coincidence and they sent officers to question the suspect about the murder. Meanwhile, the suspect's sister secured the services of a lawyer to represent her brother on the burglary charge. Neither she nor the lawyer knew about the suspicions concerning the unsolved murder case. The lawyer telephoned the police station and said she would come to the station to be present if the police wished to question her client. The lawyer was told that the police would not question him until the following morning and she could come to the station at that time. Meanwhile, the police from the other city arrived and initiated the first of a series of evening questioning sessions with the suspect. The suspect was not informed that his sister had obtained the services of a lawyer to represent him. The suspect was not told that the lawyer had called the police and asked to be present during any questioning. During questioning, the suspect was informed of his Miranda rights, waived his right to be represented by counsel during questioning, and subsequently confessed to the murder. (Courts, Criminal Law)

    a.    If you were the defense attorney, what arguments would you make to have the confession excluded from evidence?

    b.    If you were the judge, would you permit the confession to be used in evidence? Provide reasons for your decision.

31. Divide the class into small groups (5 or so students each). Each group is assigned the task of designing the curriculum for a **police training program** run by a major city for its newly hired police officers. Each group must decide what subjects will be taught in the training program, how they will be taught, and how much time will be spent on each subject. The design of the training program should reflect each group's conception of what a police officer's job entails. Appropriate time and attention should be paid to each required subject according to the importance of that subject to the performance of an officer's duties.

When the groups have developed their ideas, the entire class can compare each group's curriculum design. When examining each proposal, consider whether the contents of the curriculum reflect elements of James Q. Wilson's **policing styles: Watchman, Legalistic, and Service.**

Compare the emphasis each group gave to subjects such as criminal investigations, weapons and marksmanship, and arrest procedures. Consider whether subjects such as race relations, first aid, substance abuse, mediation, and interpersonal communications have been underemphasized or omitted. Which of the subjects should be taught in a classroom lecture/discussion context? Should any subjects be taught through role-playing, field observation, and other participatory techniques? In discussing the curriculum proposals, students should confront the gaps that may exist between public perceptions about police officers as **crime fighters** and the reality of the predominance of police officers' **service and order maintenance responsibilities**.

32. Ask the students to develop an interview instrument to be used by police officers in **interviewing victims of domestic violence**.

What questions should be asked and what information should be conveyed in the course of the police officer's interaction with a victim? In examining the questions developed by the students, attention should be paid to the role implications and objectives of particular questions selected for use. Do the questions (and information to be conveyed to the victim) reflect a **service orientation or a law enforcement orientation**? Are there special issues of sensitivity that will require questions to be asked in a certain way? What does this exercise show about the difficulties involved in encounters between **the police and citizens**? (Criminal Investigation, Victimology)

33. Exercise: **The Organization of the Police**

   Imagine that you are a member of Congress. One of your staff assistants brings you a proposal to nationalize law enforcement throughout the United States. The proposal calls for abolishing state police agencies, county sheriffs, and local police departments. Instead, Congress would create a new U.S. Department of Law Enforcement. A Secretary of Law Enforcement would oversee a national police agency which would have units established in each state, county, city, and town. Your assistant argues that the new organization would save resources by coordinating the work of every law enforcement officer in the nation and creating a standard set of law enforcement policies and priorities. In addition, the plan would standardize training, salary, and benefits for police officers everywhere and thus raise the level of **professionalism of police**, especially in small towns and rural areas.

   Before you decide whether or not to present this proposal to Congress, respond to the following questions.

   a.   Are there any undesirable consequences that could develop from putting this plan into action?

   b.   As a politician, you are concerned about how others will react to the plan. How do you think each group would react and why?

      ▪   Voters
      ▪   State and local politicians
      ▪   Police officers

c.   Will you support the proposal? Why or why not?

34. Exercise: **Police Policy**

You are a retired police chief. A state government has hired you to provide advice on the appropriate police policy to implement in several jurisdictions. You advise them on whether to choose the **watchman, legalistic, or service style**. Explain why.

a.   A city of 100,000 that contains a diverse mixture of Whites, African-Americans, Asian-Americans, and Hispanics. The unemployment rate is high. Few wealthy people live in the city. Most people are middle-class, but 25 percent of the citizens qualify for government assistance. The police department reflects the racial/ethnic mix of the city's population.

b.   A small town of 2,000 residents. Most residents work in one lumber mill or in businesses that serve loggers and farmers who live in the area. The town's population is almost entirely white, except when large numbers of people from various minority groups arrive in the summer and fall to work on local farms.

c.   A suburb with 15,000 residents. Twenty percent of the residents are members of minority groups. Nearly all of the town's residents are white-collar or professional workers with high incomes. Most people commute to a big city to work.

35. **Becoming a Police Officer**: Ask several of the students who are seeking a career in law enforcement to act as panelists and the remaining students to serve as an audience. Begin a question-answer exchange where you interview the panelists about their motivations for wanting to become police officers.

36. Divide the class into small groups and have the students address the issue of **women as police officers**. Should women be held to the same physical standards (height, weight, and strength requirements) as men in becoming police officers? In what ways might women actually be better at policing?

37. Divide the class into small groups. Each group is to act as consultants to a police department. The student must develop

proposals to address issues of **police isolation and stress**. These proposals might involve training, interaction with others in the community, individual counseling, or any other approach that the students may develop. After the proposals are developed and presented, analyze their likely effectiveness. Discuss how the nature of police work and interactions of police with citizens in conflict-laden, stressful situations makes it difficult to see how issues of stress and isolation can be eliminated.

38. Have the students interview a police officer. Require the students report on the **organization** of the police department as well as its **bureaucracy**. (Careers)

39. Have a number of students participate in a ride along with local police and then have them report their experiences to the entire class. What did the students learn about **police response and action** from the ride along? Did it change their perception of police work at all? How?

40. Divide the class into small groups and have the students debate the constitutionality of **DNA** "fingerprinting." Does this violate the right to privacy? How could DNA information be used unethically? Ask the students if they favor DNA use by police. What are the advantages and disadvantages? (Criminal Investigation, Criminal Law)

41. Exercise: **Recruitment and Training of Police Officers** (Careers)

    a. What qualifications would you require for someone to be hired as a police officer? Why?

    b. What salary and benefits would you offer in order to attract the police officer-candidates that you described?

    c. What are the three most important subjects that should be taught to new police recruits? Why?

    d. Could you use training to combat any negative aspects of the police subculture and working personality? If so, how?

42. Have the students debate the meaning of the terms "probable cause," "reasonable suspicion," and "unreasonable search and seizure." Students should come to a variety of conclusions regarding these terms which can be used to illustrate the discretion

available to police officers in the area of **search and seizure**. (Criminal Investigation)

43. Have the students debate the limits of the **plain view doctrine** as well as the plain feel and other senses. Where should the line be drawn? (Criminal Investigation)

44. Have the students discuss the variety of **warrantless searches** that are legal under case law established by the U. S. Supreme Court. Should the Court expand warrantless searches into other areas in light of the "War on Terrorism?" (Criminal Investigation, Terrorism and Homeland Security, Criminal Law)

45. Divide the students into teams to prepare arguments about **constitutional issues affecting police practices**. Two teams can square off against each other to debate the proposition: The exclusionary rule is necessary to ensure that people's rights are protected against unreasonable searches and seizures.

Another set of teams can debate each other about the proposition: Miranda warnings are not necessary because they are not actually required by the Constitution and they do little to protect criminal suspects. In the course of examining these issues, the students may be forced to see more clearly both sides of the continuing debates about these important criminal justice issues. (Criminal Investigation, Criminal Law)

46. Exercise: **The Justification for Warrantless Searches**

Warrantless searches are important for police officers in regard to gathering evidence that might otherwise be lost or endanger the safety of others in society. In the following exercise, students should list the basis for justifying the warrantless searches listed below. (Criminal Investigation, Criminal Law)

    a. What purpose(s) are served by allowing law enforcement officers to conduct a search without a warrant?

    b. Are these searches justified in violating a person's rights based upon the purposes that you listed?

- Stop and Frisk on the Streets
- Warrantless Search of Hispanics 5 miles from the Mexican border

- Search Incident to a Lawful Arrest
- Automobile Searches
- Searching through someone's luggage at the airport
- Consent searches

47. Divide the class into small groups. Each group is to act as consultants to a police department. The student must develop proposals to address issues of **police patrolling**. These proposals might involve training, interaction with others in the community, or any other approach that the students may develop. After the proposals are developed and presented, analyze their likely effectiveness.

48. Divide the class into small groups. Each group is to act as a committee within a state legislature. In the aftermath of the Rodney King case in 1992, in which police officers were convicted on federal civil rights charges after being videotaped while beating a motorist who had been speeding, citizens in your state have complained that there is inadequate control over police who use **excessive force**. These special legislative committees are assigned the task of recommending procedures and remedies to handle citizens' complaints about the police. The committee has four specific proposals to consider. They may recommend that the legislature enact any or all of these proposals, or they can develop alternative proposals to recommend to the legislature. (Ethics)

a. Proposal #1: All counties, cities, and towns will be required to develop **internal review boards** within law enforcement agencies. These review boards will be composed of both senior officers and patrol officers. In response to complaints from citizens about specific officers, the boards will investigate the complaints and may take testimony from victims, witnesses, and police officers. The boards will issue findings and recommendations to the local police chief or county sheriff. If the findings are against the officer, the officer will have the opportunity to appeal to the local police chief or county sheriff before punishments, ranging from letter of reprimand to suspension to dismissal, are imposed by the police chief or sheriff.

b. Proposal #2: All counties, cities, and towns will develop **citizen review boards** to evaluate complaints from citizens concerning law enforcement officers. The review boards will be comprised of citizens appointed by the local county, city, or town council. The review board will investigate citizen complaints and will take testimony from victims, witnesses, and police officers. The board will make findings and disciplinary recommendations to the local county, city, or town council. If the findings are against the law enforcement officer, the officer may appeal to the local county, city, or town council before the council imposes punishment.

c. Proposal #3: The state legislature shall enact a law making law enforcement officers personally liable for damages caused by the excessive use of force. Plaintiffs must show by a preponderance of evidence that excessive force was used.

d. Proposal #4: The state legislature shall enact a law making counties, cities, and towns liable for damages caused by their police officers' excessive use of force. Plaintiffs must show evidence beyond a reasonable doubt that excessive force was used.

In discussing these alternatives, the small groups should consider which constituencies will favor which proposals and the potential consequences of each proposal. For example, will an internal review board favor police officers' accounts of events over the testimony by citizen witnesses? Should citizens, like police officers, have the opportunity to appeal the board's decisions if they disagree with them? Will a citizen review board attempt to interfere with police operations and policies in ways that police officers view as detrimental to their law enforcement functions? How will police officers respond to Proposal #3 in which a jury can potentially bankrupt them by second-guessing a judgment that they made in the heat of a stressful conflict situation during an arrest or other incident? Can any citizen meet the standard of proof required under Proposal #4 ("beyond a reasonable doubt") in order to receive compensation from the government? It is difficult to strike a careful balance between protecting police officers' discretionary judgments from undue second-guessing and preventing the use of excessive force.

49. **Police accountability**: Debate in class with the students the best methods to hold police accountable. Are there any alternatives that are not listed in the textbook? (Ethics)

50. Divide the students into groups. Each group is to serve as consultants to the owner of a new casino. The students must develop a **security plan** for the casino. They must include in their plan a description of the security jobs required at the casino, the kinds of people who will be hired for such jobs, and how these people will be trained and supervised.

51. Exercise: **Patrol Strategies**

    You are the police chief in a medium-sized city. In one residential neighborhood, citizens are alarmed (and complaining to city hall) because there has been a rash of burglaries. In the downtown area, an increase in muggings has the merchants concerned about losing business. At a city council meeting, representatives from both groups ask you how you can adjust patrol strategies to address the problems in each area.

    Pretend that you are responding to their questions in explaining below how each patrol strategy might impact (or not impact) the two problems areas in the city.

    a. **Preventive Patrol**
    b. **Foot Patrol**
    c. **Aggressive Patrol**

    Whether or not you would adopt any of the foregoing patrol strategies, describe how you would address the crime problems in each area in order to reduce the problem and/or make the citizens feel less concerned.

52. Are any **community policing strategies** being used in your community? If so, which ones? Answers will vary. This would make a good research project.

53. How might the historical role of the police in enforcing slavery in the South and later segregation contribute to present-day **police-minority relations**?

54. Have you witnessed any examples of the "**thin blue line**?" Have students share their personal experiences.

55. Have students find an article on **community policing** and outline it. Ask them to be prepared to discuss their reaction to the article with the class.

56. What is the image of the police in your community? What factors are responsible for this image? Could the **police image** be made more positive? Is the image based on stereotypes? Do students know any officers personally? How has that changed their opinion? This is a good place to discuss negative contacts with police.

57. **Police ethics**: Are police officers now more violent and less ethical than their predecessors? Would the Rodney King incident have been more or less likely to have occurred 25 years ago? Have the class discuss this.

58. How do you explain the development of the two contradictory models in policing: **community-oriented policing (COP) and special weapons and tactics (SWAT) teams**? Can they coexist?

59. What should be a department's ideal balance between **fighting crime and service** to the community?

60. Have you witnessed police exercise their discretion? How did it impress you? Anyone who has received a traffic ticket or only a warning has experienced **police discretion**. (Ethics)

61. What decisions commonly made by police officers involve **ethical considerations**? Answers will vary but could include truthfulness in court (especially when the accused might go free on a technicality) declining gifts, gratuities and "police discounts," and how suspects in their custody will be treated. (Ethics)

62. Have students research and outline at least one of the following topics: **mission statement, police discretion, police culture, police ethics or police corruption**.

63. Use the Internet to locate a police department' website you are interested in and write down their **mission statement**.

64. What instances of **broken windows** have you seen in your neighborhood? Other neighborhoods? Examples might include uncollected trash, abandoned homes and buildings, tall grass and weeds, graffiti, potholes in the streets, broken streetlights.

65. How extensively are the services of **private security** used in your community? Do they cooperate with or compete against the local police? Have students check the yellow pages and invite a representative of private security to class to speak.

66. Which seems more "just" to you: **retributive justice** or **restorative justice**? (Ethics)

67. Use your telephone directory to determine what **city services** and **community resources** are available. Select one to contact and to determine what relationship (if any) exists between it and your local police department.

68. Does your police department use **problem solving**? Check with your local police department. If they do, find out when they began using it and whether they think it is more effective than traditional policing.

69. Does your law enforcement agency employ anyone to specifically conduct **crime analysis**? Have students research this by checking with the local police department.

70. How might **computers** help police in their **problem-solving** efforts?

71. Have students find an example of a **police-community partnership** that successfully used problem solving to deal with community issues. Suggest that students might also see the Community Policing Consortium at www.communitypolicing.org, the Police Executive Research Forum at www.PoliceForum.org, or other community policing sites.

72. Have students research at least one of the following subjects: **crime mapping, geographic profiling, or problem-oriented policing**. Ask students to take good notes and to be prepared to share them in class.

73. Select and research a chronic problem that exists in your community. Form a problem-solving team with classmates, assign appropriate roles (police, business owner, school official, residents, etc.), and using the **SARA problem-solving model**, develop solutions.

74. **Crime Assessment**: How would you go about assessing your community's needs regarding efforts to reduce crime and violence? The students might survey the citizens and officers. Crime records, accident reports and other calls for service may show what a community's needs are regarding crime and violence.

75. **Police-Community Relations:** Have students research and take notes on how an administrator can build support within the police department and the community.

76. **Police-Community Relations:** Conduct a community survey of business owners or campus or neighborhood residents. Ask about:

    a.  Their fear of crime
    b.  Their opinion of police services in their community
    c.  What they think community policing means
    d.  Whether they believe their police or sheriff's department practices community policing
    e.  If they could decide, what would they direct the police to concentrate on?

77. Why is trust an issue between police and residents of low-income neighborhoods? **Mistrust of police** may have a long history in poorer communities.

78. Does your local police department have a **press information officer?**

79. How fairly do you feel the **media** in your community report crime and violence? Collect three examples to support your position. Watch television news reports and check newspaper accounts for balance in reporting and editorials. It might be interesting to ask this question of police officers, public defenders, and prosecutors.

80. How fairly do you feel **national media** (radio, television, magazines, newspapers) cover crime and violence? Collect three examples to support your position. Watch television news reports and check newspaper accounts for balance in reporting and editorials. Have students discuss who they think is doing the better job – local or national media.

81. Driven by TV ratings or newspaper sales, **media news coverage** has become almost completely crime reporting. Insensitivity

toward victims, close-up photos of carnage, revelation of sensitive case facts or of suspects and often just plain poor taste have many Americans fed up with the media. Reporters have accompanied officers on arrest warrant services, ridden along with officers and photographed police work in-progress. Have students research crime reporting and have a small group or entire class discussion about the pros and cons of the current sensational atmosphere around crime and the media and how it affects perceptions of the crime situation and **fear of crime**.

82. Examine a weeks' worth of local **media crime reporting** (newspaper and television). How often do crime stories lead? Do they appear sensationalized? Are crime stories overrepresented?

83. If possible, interview a local crime reporter and a police department representative about **crime reporting** in your city. How does the reporting relate to the level of crime?

84. Why would a police department want to reduce **fear of crime** rather than crime itself? Fear of crime is often exaggerated, especially among the older population. Fearful people often become prisoners in their own homes, withdrawing from community life and leaving the streets to be taken over by the criminal element. Also, fearful people usually look vulnerable and, hence, may become so.

85. How much of a police department's budget should be devoted to **police policy research**? Which areas should be of highest priority? Contact the local police department to learn how much of their budget is devoted to research. For departments with little or no budget, what alternatives exist? For example, university students or crime prevention association volunteers might conduct surveys of police effectiveness in the community.

86. What **police-community relations programs** does your local police department participate in?

87. What **crime prevention programs** are in your community? Have the students participated in any of them?

88. One of the most effective and least expensive security initiatives is to design and build safety from crime and fear of crime into a

structure. Have students research **CPTED** and discuss how the following can affect crime and/or fear of crime...

a. Smell and sound
b. Parking garages
c. Maintenance
d. Color
e. Mix of activities
f. Restrooms
g. Signage
h. Vehicle – pedestrian conflicts
i. Loitering
j. "Hanging out"

89. Do you have any "**broken windows**" in your community? If so, how would you characterize them? What might be done to mend them?

90. Conduct a survey of a portion of your institution's campus and determine whether any of the **CPTED** principles might make that portion of campus safer.

91. **Police and Juveniles:** How did you feel about the police when you were a child? Did that attitude change as you grew older? Why or why not and, if so, how?

92. **Police Policy Development:** The chief of police of Our Town receives a letter from the prosecutor stating that a serious problem exists in prosecuting DUI cases because there is no uniformity of procedures. To correct this, a policy must be written and instituted to successfully prosecute cases and to reinstate the faith of the public. This news comes as a shock to the chief, who immediately asks you as supervisor of the traffic division to take charge. The chief emphasizes that this is a problem demanding immediate attention. DUI cases must be thoroughly investigated so offenders can be successfully prosecuted.

Instructions: Write a procedure so officers who deal with DUI have direction, guidance and technical information. Include ways of detecting a driver under the influence, probable cause for stopping, observing the driver's condition, questioning the driver, giving the necessary field tests and invoking the implied consent law. Officers should mentally record the events as they occur as accurately as possible and make written notes at the earliest practical time. Witnesses should be interviewed to strengthen the case.

93. Do you view **discretion** as more of an advantage or a disadvantage for police officers?

Students may differ on this debatable subject. It is always good dialogue to know what viewpoints and differences exist when it comes to police discretion. A lively discussion can ensue.

94. Have you observed **police discretion** in operation?

Here students should convey either their own experiences or knowledge they may have acquired through friends.

95. **Advising of Rights:** How would you warn a suspect of his rights if, while you were interviewing this person, he suddenly said, "I committed the crime"?

Spontaneous remarks by an individual admitting to a crime have been upheld by the courts as admissible evidence. After the admission, the officer then should advise the suspect of his or her rights.

96. What are some positive outcomes of good **incident reports**?

Positive results of good incident reports include providing a permanent record of facts, providing a basis for prosecution, and providing documentation of present, past and potential future service needs. Good reports are understood by other members of the department and are embraced by prosecuting attorneys, who have limited time and must have a factual, understandable report from the officers to determine if warrants or charges ought to be made. The legal system encourages officers to make good reports so everyone involved may come to faster conclusions.

97. How do the **media** affect police operations?

Since most of what the public knows about law enforcement comes from mass media, their opinion and support is vital to an agency.

98. The **Fifth Amendment** provides that no person shall be "deprived of life, liberty or property without due process of law." What does this really mean? Explain your answer as if you were giving a lecture to a high school class.

The answer to this question could fill a book. The Fifth Amendment to the U.S. Constitution has been the focal point for hundreds of Supreme Court decisions in part because of its vagueness. Like other clauses in the Bill of Rights, the guarantees found in the Fifth Amendment are not self-defining and require judicial interpretation. The Fifth Amendment has three clauses: the guarantee against double jeopardy, the privilege against self-incrimination and the requirements in federal courts of grand jury indictments. These are important to the criminal process.

99. Describe a good example of "**reasonable grounds of suspicion**."

Reasonable grounds for suspicion is a series of circumstances that allow an officer to believe a crime has been committed or is about to be committed. For example, an unoccupied car is running outside a convenience store, shots are fired, and a man runs out of the store with a fistful of money. A police officer could reasonably infer a robbery has occurred. What could be wrong with this assumption?

100. Do you feel that given the awesome power police hold, they can ever be true partners with citizens in **community policing**?

The police get their power from the people in some manner or another, through laws, constitutions and community privileges. To maintain order in a community, there must always be a police presence that also has police power. True partnerships are the desired goal but a goal that is most difficult to achieve.

101. Using the Internet, search for *patrol* and note the abundance of types listed. Select a law enforcement-related site and outline the information presented on the home page.

102. Using the Internet, search *for **community policing*** and select two of the sites to review. Compare the types of programs and initiatives being used in each department and note reasons why they may be similar or different. How does the population,

geography, socioeconomic climate, etc, factor in? Be prepared to share your findings with the class.

103. Which is the most effective method of **patrol**: foot patrol, bicycle patrol, one-officer patrol vehicle, two-officer patrol vehicle or some other method?

Community policing is becoming very popular. Community policing reaches out to the community with the officers assuming more foot patrol duty. It is thought that by having more contact with the people in the community, a certain amount of crime might be controlled. Researchers are awaiting results that might influence the future of policing.

104. What are the relative strengths and weaknesses of **foot patrol and automobile patrol**? How can these two patrol methods be combined to enhance the effectiveness of patrol efforts?

Foot patrol limits officers' ability to move around quickly and limits response time to calls for service. Automobile patrol takes the officer away from close contact with the population but adds a dimension of quick response to calls, particularly emergency calls. The automobile also allows carrying necessary equipment to do the job adequately.

105. **Police Organization:** You have been appointed the new commissioner of the Anycity Police Department. Anycity is a suburban city, 60 miles from a major U.S. city, with a population of 30,000 people, and a police department of 100 officers. The major police problems in Anycity are disorderly teens making unnecessary noise at night, parking and traffic problems in Anycity's commercial district during business hours and daytime residential burglaries.

The former commissioner's assistant informs you that the department has no organization chart, no written rules and procedures, and has, "always done a great job in the past".

Anycity's City Manager however, tells you that the former commissioner was an "incompetent" and that the department is totally disorganized and ineffective. You review the department's personnel records and find that, of the 100 officers in the department, 30% are patrol officers, 30% are detectives, and 40%

are supervisors. Additionally, the entire department is divided evenly into the three tours of duty.

In view of what you learned in this chapter - Would you re-organize the department? Why or Why not? If you would, how would you do it?

106. What is the **police culture or subculture** and how does it manifest itself?

107. Describe the **police personality**. Does police work attract people who already have this personality or is it the result of becoming an officer?

108. What is the **Dirty Harry Problem**? Could you ever justify an officer acting the way Dirty Harry Callahan did? Why or Why Not?

109. What are some of the methods being used by police departments today in order to deal with **police stress**?

110. **Minority Relations:** Why have police departments historically had a poor relationship with the African-American community? (Race)

111. Name and describe some programs police departments have initiated between **special populations of citizens**. Which one of them do you believe offers the best service to a special population group? (Race)

112. Name and describe several **community crime prevention programs**. Select one which you believe offers the most potential in reducing and preventing crime and explain your rationale.

113. What is the rationale behind **DARE programs**? (Juvenile Justice)

114. You are the president of the city of Smalltown's police community council, a group of citizens who work with the police to improve the quality of life and the quality of **police - citizen relationships** in Smalltown. Two days ago a Smalltown police officer was captured on a video camera brutally beating a Smalltown resident, who remained motionless on the ground. The tape was turned over to a local cable station which has played it numerous times each day, causing many residents to complain openly of police brutality

and harassment. Smalltown police officers have reported that numerous teens are screaming insults at them as they pass in their police cars. One officer reported that a teenager openly challenged him to a fight.

The police chief has called the community council into session and asks for advice in correcting the rapidly deteriorating relationship between the police and the community.

What would be your recommendations to the chief?

115. How does the **Bill of Rights** and the actions of the **United States Supreme Court** regulate the police?

116. Your younger brother, a high school sophomore, brags to his Future Government Leaders Club, that you know everything there is to know about the United States Supreme Court. The club's faculty advisor calls you and asks you to participate in a debate at a future club meeting. The subject to be debated is: "The Supreme Court of the 1980s and 1990s has swung too far to the right by over-emphasizing the rights of society and under-emphasizing **individual rights.**" He asks you which side you wish to take, and tells you to be prepared to quote as many cases as possible in the area of **search and seizure**, and **custodial interrogation**, to defend your stand.

117. You have been appointed the Personnel Director of the City of Anywhere, U.S.A. Anywhere, with a population of 60,000 has a police department of 120 officers. There are currently no **female officers** on the department, and the department is expected to lose 30 officers through retirement this year. The local chapter of the National Organization of Women (NOW) is claiming that Anywhere is discriminating against females in its police hiring process. Develop a comprehensive plan to increase female representation in the department. (Women)

118. Last year you successfully passed your local police department's entrance examination. During this year you have successfully passed the department's physical agility, psychological, and medical examination and its background investigation. This morning you received a letter in the mail from the police department telling you that you have been accepted for

appointment and advising you to report to City Hall next Monday to be sworn in as a probationary police officer.

You have never told your parents about your plans to become a police officer because you were sure they would object since they consider police work to be an extremely dangerous occupation. Now you must tell your mother, an accountant, and your father, a high school English teacher that you will be becoming a police officer. You are sure that they are going to be very upset about your decision and very fearful of your future safety. Before you talk to them, think about what you will tell them about the degree of **danger in police work**.

119. Have the class watch the 1973 movie, *Serpico*. After the movie, break the class up into discussion groups. Ask the groups to discuss such topics as the **blue curtain subculture, ethics, Internal Affairs, and discretion.** (Ethics)

120. Much of the discussion on **police profiling** in this chapter centers on studies that have examined this practice with black and Latino citizens. In light of today's terrorist concerns and military actions, to what extent is profiling an issue for citizens from the Middle East? (Terrorism and Homeland Security)

121. Students always express interest in the ability of police officers to stop and **search** their automobiles. Have students discuss the circumstances under which this occurred to them and then discuss the legal issues that made this an appropriate response for the officer. (Criminal Law)

122. Have a local member of your police department speak to your class about **routine activity theory** and its application to **community policing.** (Criminology)

123. Have the local DARE officer come in to discuss the **DARE program** in your community. (Juvenile Justice, Drugs)

124. Have the local Community Policing Officer come talk to your class about what the police department is doing to help **juveniles**. (Juvenile Justice)

# Criminal Investigation

1. If you are fortunate enough to have a **state crime lab** nearby, either arrange for the students to visit the lab, or have a representative come to class and discus things such as **DNA testing, AFIS**, etc.

2. If your local police department uses **crime mapping**, invite an officer to come to class and explain its usefulness for the department. (Policing)

3. Many police departments have detectives who analyze the blood patterns at crime scenes. Invite such an analyst to come to class and explain **how blood spatter pattern** help solve crimes.

4. Ask the students to develop an interview instrument to be used by police officers in **interviewing victims** of domestic violence.

   What questions should be asked and what information should be conveyed in the course of the police officer's interaction with a victim? In examining the questions developed by the students, attention should be paid to the role implications and objectives of particular questions selected for use. Do the questions (and information to be conveyed to the victim) reflect a service orientation or a law enforcement orientation? Are there special issues of sensitivity that will require questions to be asked in a certain way? What does this exercise show about the difficulties involved in encounters between the police and citizens? (Policing, Victimization)

5. Divide the class into small groups and have the students debate the constitutionality of **DNA** "fingerprinting." Does this violate the right to privacy? How could DNA information be used unethically? Ask the students if they favor DNA use by police. What are the advantages and disadvantages? (Policing, Criminal Law)

6. Have the students debate the meaning of the terms "probable cause," "reasonable suspicion," and "unreasonable search and seizure." Students should come to a variety of conclusions regarding these terms which can be used to illustrate the discretion

available to police officers in the area of **search and seizure**. (Policing)

7. Have the students debate the limits of the **plain view doctrine** as well as the plain feel and other senses. Where should the line be drawn? (Policing)

8. Have the students discuss the variety of **warrantless searches** that are legal under case law established by the U. S. Supreme Court. Should the Court expand warrantless searches into other areas in light of the "War on Terrorism?" (Policing, Terrorism and Homeland Security, Criminal Law)

9. Divide the students into teams to prepare arguments about **constitutional issues affecting police practices**. Two teams can square off against each other to debate the proposition: The exclusionary rule is necessary to ensure that people's rights are protected against unreasonable searches and seizures. Another set of teams can debate each other about the proposition: Miranda warnings are not necessary because they are not actually required by the Constitution and they do little to protect criminal suspects. In the course of examining these issues, the students may be forced to see more clearly both sides of the continuing debates about these important criminal justice issues. (Policing, Criminal Law)

10. Exercise: **The Justification for Warrantless Searches**

   Warrantless searches are important for police officers in regard to gathering evidence that might otherwise be lost or endanger the safety of others in society. In the following exercise, students should list the basis for justifying the warrantless searches listed below. (Policing, Criminal Law)

   a. What purpose(s) are served by allowing law enforcement officers to conduct a search without a warrant?

   b. Are these searches justified in violating a person's rights based upon the purposes that you listed?

      ▪ Stop and Frisk on the Streets
      ▪ Warrantless Search of Hispanics five miles from the Mexican border
      ▪ Search Incident to a Lawful Arrest

- Automobile Searches
- Searching through someone's luggage at the airport
- Consent searches

11. Debate whether a **DNA database** should be developed to solve crime more rapidly. What are the implications in terms of privacy and constitutional rights? (Criminal Law)

12. Conduct a keyword search of *criminal investigation*. This will take you to many informative and educational abstracts, beneficial not only to students but also to practicing police officers. Select one abstract to review and outline. Be prepared to share your outline with the class.

13. Discuss the many ways the **computer** is revolutionalizing police work. ( Forensics and Technology)

14. What is **DNA**? What is its status in America's court system today?

15. Complete a search of the WWW and list five federal agencies that handle **criminal investigations**.

16. Search for state agencies in two states and describe the **criminal investigative responsibilities** that the agency has for criminal investigations.

17. Search the NCJRS (National Criminal Justice Reference Service) web site for **Crime Mapping**. In one page, describe crime mapping, using the publications as a reference.

18. In a traditional class discussion, have the class members list the reasons why **patrol officers** have a difficult time following up on more complex criminal investigations.

19. Search the below web sites for information on **crime scene sketches and photographs** and then complete the following tasks. Review what they contain concerning sketches and photographs and be prepared to discuss the differences and why you believe the differences exist.

    a.   http://www.crime-scene-investigator.net/csi-photo.html
    b.   http://www.geocities.com/cfpdlab/csphoto.html
    c.   http://www.fbi.gov/hq/lab/handbook/intro16.htm
    d.   http://www.ncjrs.org/txtfiles1/nij/178280.txt

20. In a traditional classroom discussion, ask students to list the ways that **weather** may pose a challenge to investigation and how investigators might overcome the problems of wind, rain and snow.

21. For **report-writing tips**, view the following site:

    http://www.policemag.com/t_dutytips.cfm?rank=91352

    Have the class use the internet to search for a recent major crime in the community. Have the students write a report based on the newspaper account of the incident, using an outline process.

22. Bring in a newspaper report of a recent crime in the community. Describe the article to the class members and have them discuss what the most important elements of the case are and how they would write a **report** for investigators.

23. Set up a **mock crime scene** that allows the students to search for evidence of a crime. If time permits, use an indoor and an outdoor crime scene. The students are to identify the nature of the search pattern they used and why. Tell the students that the crime involves an assault with a knife. If time for a mock crime scene does not exist then have a class discussion of what the students would do to process the crime scene.

24. Have the class discuss issues with the finding and submission of evidence. What problems might an investigator encounter in collecting and submitting **blood stains** for analysis? (Forensics and Technology)

25. Go to the website of the Federal Bureau of Investigation (http://www.fbi.gov/) and search for articles about **interviews and interrogations.** Review the articles and select two major points from the articles.

26. Discuss the various issues related to **interviews and interrogations** with the class. Have the class members list the different tactics they would use in an interview versus an interrogation of a suspect.

27. Have class members split into pairs and take turns playing the role of a victim and an investigator, then of a suspect and an interrogator, for a limited period of time. Afterwards, have the

class members discuss what they learned, both while playing the **investigator/interrogator role** and observing their partner in it.

28. Have the class members discuss what steps they would take to **develop, identify, and pursue suspects** in the following case, as well as what measures they would implement in order to prevent these incidents from recurring:

Two men have been shot to death and five others injured during a violent weekend confrontation in a local bar called Sid's. Preliminary evidence suggests that it is the result of tensions between two rival motorcycle gangs, the Mad Dogs and the Wild Cats, known to be active in the area. A number of battles involving fatalities have taken place across the country between sections of these two gangs in recent months. The confrontation seems to have erupted after the discovery of the body of Jack Harvey early Saturday. Harvey, who was found shot to death in a ditch roughly 50 miles outside of town, was discovered wearing a jacket with a Mad Dog insignia on it.

Police have one man in custody, Alvin Smith, and have charged him with murder in connection with the battle. The major evidence linking him to the shooting is a surveillance videotape, which shows portions of the battle, including a man police have identified as Smith firing several shots from a revolver. However, the firearm has not been recovered, and the sequence of events on the videotape is not clear. The tape contains defects and shifts in perspective that make reconstructing what happened more difficult, and a thorough analysis could take months. Smith is believed to be a member of the Mad Dogs, and the first dead man, who died at the scene, is a confirmed member of the Wild Cats. The other victim, who died at the hospital, was not a local resident, and his gang affiliations, if any, are still unknown. Of the five injured men, one (a Mad Dog) is unconscious and has suffered brain damage; two (one Wild Cat and one Mad Dog) are in stable condition; and two (one Wild Cat, and one apparently uninvolved person) are in good condition.

29. Have students go to the FBI website at http://www.fbi.gov/ and perform a search on the word "**murder**." Ask them to select three

cases from the results provided and discuss what they might learn by examining the body of the victim. (Forensics and Technology)

30. Have students discuss the issues that would confront a **homicide investigator** in the following cases.

    a.    A farmer has found a greatly decomposed body in one of his fields. While plowing the field for the first time in two years, he ran over the body and the plow brought the body to the surface.

    b.    A male, aged 20 to 40, has been found in an alley in the bar area of town. There is no obvious cause of death. The body was found when a janitor came out of a bar at approximately 4:00 a.m. When the officers arrived at the scene they checked for signs of life and cancelled the ambulance. At that time, according to the responding officer, the body was warm to the touch, about 40 degrees. Based on what appear to be scuff marks, it is possible that the body was dragged into the alley.

    c.    A female, aged approximately 15 to 25, has been found in a fraternity bedroom. The victim is lying on her side on the bed. The responding officers have learned that the fraternity had a party the night before and that she was one of the students at the party. The bedroom is a mess, but this might or might not indicate a struggle, as other rooms in the same hallway are also disordered. However, some of the bed covers are on the floor, which may indicate that something out of the ordinary went on. There is no visible blood in the room.

31. Have students review the **American Bar Association** (ABA) website (http://www.abanet.org/domviol/areyou.html) and answer the following questions, either individually in written form, or during a class discussion.

    a.    What does the ABA recommend for **victims of domestic violence**?

    b.    Are there any differences between what the ABA recommends and what the text recommends?

32. Have class members discuss the issues of **domestic violence** and how best to respond to the following case.

A male who seems tired and disoriented is found wandering along a side street. The officer brings the male to the police station in order to determine the best course of action. The male is informed that he is not under arrest, just that the officer is taking him to the department so that he can be more comfortable. On the way to the station and at the station, the male recounts being assaulted by his wife. He does state that he has hit her once or twice during their marriage, but has "only slapped her." He says that he has not had any recent altercations with her, but that earlier today, while he was in bed, she hit him over the head repeatedly with a hard object that he believes may have been a metal cooking pan. He says that he remembers very little between the time of this assault and the time he was picked up by the officer on the street.

His story has some unusual aspects and seems to run counter to a number of trends observed in domestic violence. However, this does not necessarily mean that the events described by the man did not occur. What actions would you take as the officer in this case?

33. Ask students to navigate to...

    http://www.fbi.gov/publications/leb/2002/jan02leb.pdf

    and read "Police and Sexual Assault," by Craig Wilson, published in the FBI Bulletin in January 2002.

    Have them write a short paper about the steps they would take to implement the **Sexual Assault Team** model in their own community.

34. **Types of cases:** Have the class discuss the different issues that may arise in cases involving:

    a.   A male victim of sexual assault.
    b.   Juvenile victims of sexual assault.
    c.   Older victims of sexual assault (65 and over).

35. Have the class discuss the methods they might use to apprehend the members of a **child sexual pornography ring**.

36. Have students search the World Wide Web for suggestions from security firms and consultants about how bank employees and other business employees should respond in the case of a **bank robbery**. Ask students to review the major points made and

determine if the suggestions offered differ from what law enforcement officers are trained to do in responding to robberies.

37. **Investigation of cases:** Describe the following cases to the class and then break the class into groups, asking them to develop suggestions for the investigation of the listed cases.

   a.  Three of the fifteen convenience stores in your community have been robbed within the last month, all between 11:00 p.m. and midnight. The same suspect, who was captured on security videotape in two of the robberies but wears a ski mask over his face, is apparently responsible for each. His modus operandi is to enter the store when it is empty, point a gun (revolver) at the clerk, and demand all the money in the cash register. The suspect speaks with a stutter and had difficulty getting the words out in one of the robberies. The clerks each say that they smelled alcohol on the suspect. What would you do?

   b.  A 24-hour-restaurant has been robbed. Shots were fired and one person was shot in the arm. Local business owners are worried and the local newspaper has carried front page articles each day for the past five days. The only evidence so far is a woolen cap that was found a block away from the store and appears similar to one worn by the robber. Some witnesses claim that the suspect seemed very nervous, and that the shots were fired when the person who was shot made a move toward the suspect. No other information exists. What would you do?

   c.  During the past week, every evening at approximately 7:00 p.m. a person on a bicycle has ridden up to a different pedestrian, pointed a knife at the individual, demanded their money and their wallet, then ridden away. In each case, the suspect has tossed the wallet on the sidewalk not far from the scene, several times in sight of the victim. The suspect has worn gloves in each case. The robberies have occurred in different parts of town and do not display a consistent pattern as to location at this point. The suspect is male and wears a bike helmet, glasses, and bike pants, as well as bike shoes of the type that snap into the peddles of the bike. He is of small

69

build and slight stature and seems to be between 20 and 30 years of age. What would you do?

38. Have students perform a web search for **burglary prevention** suggestions. Ask them to compare the content of at least two sites with the text and determine what is missing from the text and/or the web sites. Have students compile a list of suggestions for law enforcement officers based on what they read?

39. Ask students to analyze each of the **burglary cases** listed below and to indicate what actions they would take.

   a. A 35-year-old male has been arrested by patrol officers. He was caught breaking into a place of business that appeared to be deserted. However, the owner happened to be in the back office, where he had fallen asleep going over the accounts after work. The owner took a baseball bat to the suspect, knocking him out. The suspect had glass cutters, wore gloves and carried a briefcase. What type of burglar is this suspect? What actions should be taken?

   b. A 54-year-old female was arrested outside of a business when a silent alarm went off, alerting an officer in the area. He found her prying at a side door using a crowbar. While unusual in that a female has been arrested, should the investigators handle this case any differently? What actions should be taken?

   c. A 19-year-old male was arrested during a response to a home burglary in an upper-income area of the community. The youth is from a neighboring community but attends college in the town. The officers have to chase the suspect on foot and wrestle him to the ground to arrest him. He is defiant, has asked for an attorney, and claims that the officers beat him up when they arrested him. There have been a series of burglaries in the area, but each with a slightly different MO. What actions should the investigators take with this individual and the case?

40. Search the FBI's web site (http://www.fbi.gov/) for its Art Theft Program. Ask students to review the web site and write a short report about new trends in **art theft**, including new methods of

theft, new types of art thieves, types of art that seem to be increasingly targeted for theft, and new methods for preventing art theft.

41. Divide the class into groups and assign each group one specific **type of theft** (mail theft, credit card theft, art theft, etc.) discussed in the text. Ask each group to list the actions they would take as an investigator to solve the problem of their particular theft type if the same offender were committing it in more than one jurisdiction.

42. Have students search the National Highway Traffic Safety Administration website at...

    http://www.nhtsa.dot.gov/portal/site/nhtsa/menuitem.2afa3cb5b16547a1ba7d9d1046108a0c/

    Have the students look for information about **vehicle theft**, theft prevention, and related topics. Ask them to summarize the information they find and present it to the class in groups.

43. **Case solving:** Ask the students to analyze the following case in class and make suggestions to resolve it.

    There have been a series of thefts of expensive convertibles in the community. The thefts are occurring during the day. No witnesses or victims have any suspect information. In one incident the owner unknowingly observed his car being driven away, but did not realize it was his own convertible until he reached his garage to find it gone. None of the cars have been recovered. Cars are not stolen on days when there is snow on the ground. At one scene officers did find some type of debris that was consistent with parts of a convertible top. What actions would you take as an investigator?

44. Have students go to the Insurance Committee for Arson Control's website (http://www.arsoncontrol.org/) and review its suggestions for **arson control**. Ask students to summarize three major points made by the website in written form.

45. **Case solving:** Ask class members to discuss how they would handle the following cases.

    a.   The fire department has responded to a grass fire in a vacant field behind a school. They believe that several pre-teens may

71

have accidentally started a fire while playing with matches, and have asked for help with the investigation.

b.  An apartment on the fifth floor of a six-story apartment complex has been partially gutted by fire. The incident has not been definitely established as a case of arson, but two suspicious indicators exist. First, following the fire the apartment residents received an anonymous phone call from a person who stated that the fire was deliberately set. Also, the fire seems to have had two points of origin. A faint trail appears on the remnants of the living-room carpet, but it is hard to discern because of the fire damage to the carpet fibers.

c.  Following the burning of a small commercial building a week ago, the fire investigators have received an analysis of a charred floorboard that indicates the presence of accelerant on the board. The building is about 60 years old, in a middling state of repair, and has housed a number of different businesses over the years.

46. Ask students to visit the Drug Enforcement Administration's website (http://www.usdoj.gov/dea/) and review the recent major **drug cases** featured there.

Have the students each provide a short written report in which they explain the primary focus of the operations as well as any commonalities they have been able to discern in terms of where the operations have developed, how the cases have been investigated, and what issues have been involved. (Drugs)

47  Divide the class into groups and ask them to discuss the following **drug issues**: (Drugs)

a.  A highly organized group of drug sellers exists in your community. It is well-managed and efficient at evading authorities. Previous attempts to infiltrate the organization using undercover officers or informants have ended in failure, and in one case the officer was in grave danger. What other tactics might be in order?

b.  Drug sales have increased dramatically at two local high schools. What actions can local law enforcement take to reduce this problem?

c. What actions might a law enforcement agency take that would combine both enforcement and prevention of drug-related crime?

48. **Gang problems:** Have students go to the Office of Juvenile Justice Delinquency Prevention's Gang Prevention Programs website at... (Gangs)

http://www.dsgonline.com/mpg2.5/gang_prevention.htm

Ask students to review the information and provide a written report describing the steps they would take to coordinate the law enforcement response and investigations in their community with the services and programs mentioned on the site.

49. A small **juvenile gang** composed of no more than 15 members has been active in the community recently. Their members have been linked to drug sales, assaults, thefts and graffiti. The gang is multi-racial and appears to be led by a slightly older person, who is about 20 years of age. What approach would you take to reduce or eliminate these gang problems? (Gangs)

50. **Homeland Security:** Break the class into several groups and have the groups discuss answers to the following questions. (Terrorism and Homeland Security)

a. Which community organizations, governmental agencies, and other groups should be included in developing a community or hometown security plan?

b. A number of unmarried young men from the Middle East have moved into your community in recent months. What actions, if any, should be taken?

c. The Department of Homeland Security has notified you, as a member of the local police department, that a group of individuals who may be a sleeper cell for Al-Qaeda have been making drawings and taking pictures of a major bridge in your community.

51. Have students visit the portion of the website of the American Bar Association (ABA) that lists ABA standards for the prosecution of cases.

http://www.abanet.org/crimjust/standards/pfunc_toc.html

After they have reviewed these standards, ask them to respond in written form to the following questions: (Victimization, Courts)

a.   What are the ABA standards for an **extrajudicial statement**?

b.   Is a prosecutor's office expected to offer legal advice to a law enforcement agency concerning criminal matters?

c.   What is the ABA standard for **relationships with victims and witnesses** by the prosecutor?

### Forensics and Technology

1.   Invite a federal prosecutor to come to class to discuss **cybercrime** prosecution.

2.   Develop a term paper on **internet pornography** and the FBI stings that have taken place to combat it.

3.   Develop a research paper on the various types of **computer crimes**.

4.   Search for websites about **high-tech crime**. How much danger is there for the average computer user?

5.   Interview a representative of the technology (internet) provider for your school or home. Assess the representative's knowledge of **technology security** issues.

6.   Computerization and the Internet have placed new strains on law enforcement in the United States. Design a program using three strategies to prevent **cybercrime**. This assumes that prevention would be less expensive than after-the-fact apprehension and enforcement. This analysis should use concepts such as the intelligence model versus the traditional crime control model. Please justify your program in a 1,500 word essay using data and cite the sources for all data used.

7.   Discuss the many ways the **computer** is revolutionalizing police work. (Criminal Investigation)

8. Have the students create a list of possible ways **terrorists** could use **computers**. After the list has been generated, discuss the importance of counterterrorism in regards to **cyberterrorism**. (Terrorism and Homeland Security)

9. Use this link to locate the FBI Handbook of Forensic Services:

   http://www.fbi.gov/hq/lab/labhome.htm

   Review the section on **Crime Scene Safety** and provide a two-page description of the issues raised by the section.

10. Go to the Arkansas **State Crime Laboratory** web site:

    http://www.state.ar.us/crimelab/

    Review what services they offer. Determine if there are any needed additional services.

11. Have the class discuss issues with the finding and submission of evidence. What problems might an investigator encounter in collecting and submitting **blood stains** for analysis? (Criminal Investigation)

12. Have students go to the FBI website at http://www.fbi.gov/ and perform a search on the word "**murder**." Ask them to select three cases from the results provided and discuss what they might learn by examining the **body of the victim**. (Criminal Investigation)

13. Divide students into four groups. Have each group visit one of the following sites and present a detailed report to the class not only about what they learned, but about how well the site was developed, how current the information on it is, who created and maintains the site, and why investigators should (or should not) rely on the information provided.

    a. **Electronic Evidence Information Center** - http://www.e-evidence.info/

    b. **National Infrastructure Protection Center** - http://www.virtualref.com/

    c. **National White-Color Crime Center** – http://www.nctp.org/

    d. **Infobin** – www.inforbin.org/cfid/isplist.htm

14. Assign students to groups and have them discuss the following:

    a.  What steps should a law enforcement agency take to start a **computer crime unit**?

    b.  What steps should the agency take to reduce computer crime in their community?

    c.  Where would the law enforcement agency find expertise in the field that they could use to assist with the investigations?

15. Credit card abuse has become a billion dollar industry in the United States. Ask the students how many credit and debit cards they have in their name. Discuss their use in both secure and nonsecure sites on the Internet, over the telephone, and in various stores. How easy would it be for someone to gain access to their account? (Criminology)

16. The vast majority of persons with a computer connected to the Internet and e-mail have had experience with some form of a computer virus. Discuss those activities that place our personal **computers at highest risk**. What can we do to better protect our computer system? Allow the students to discuss how their computer got "infected." (Criminology)

### Terrorism and Homeland Security

1.  Ask students to recall their immediate reaction to the **9/11 attacks**.

2.  Have students prepare a debate surrounding the issues of the USA **Patriot Act**.

3.  Invite a member of the FBI to come to class to discuss the **new mission of the FBI**. (Careers)

4.  Invite members of local law enforcement agencies to come to class and discuss how they are prepared to respond to a **terrorist attack**.

5.  Have students read articles debating the pros and cons of the USA **Patriot Act**, and do oral presentations on the issue.

6. Find the Homeland Security website and identify what **public homeland security preparations have** been made in your geographic area.

7. **The Patriot Act** has certainly become a bone of contention. Please evaluate the provisions of the Act from your perspective. After reviewing The Patriot Act on the web, please address at least five issues you see as problematic. Are they assets to us or liabilities? Please justify your opinion in a 1,500 word essay using data and cite the sources for all data used.

8. Have the students discuss the variety of **warrantless searches** that are legal under case law established by the U. S. Supreme Court. Should the Court expand warrantless searches into other areas in light of the "War on Terrorism?" (Policing, Criminal Investigation, Criminal Law)

9. **Recently captured terrorists** have become classified as military non-combatants instead of prisoners of war and are thus being tried in secret military courts. As a controversial topic, should these prisoners be tried in secret in the name of national security, should they be tried in regular courts, or should the U.S. even have jurisdiction over these prisoners in lieu of some kind of international court? (Courts)

   Possible discussion points: With respect to national security, is the U.S. a vigilante? Do defendants truly meet the definition of soldier or enemy and thus become subject to the Geneva Convention?

10. Describe two terrorist events since 1994 that have had a major impact on **anti-terrorism laws**. Name one congressional act in response to each. Briefly discuss some of the provisions of these laws. (Criminal Law)

    Some main points: The bombing of the Federal Building in 1995 prompted Congress to pass the Anti-Terrorism and Effective Death Penalty Act (AEDPA). The terrorist attacks involving airliners on Sept. 11, 2001 prompted passage of the U.S.A. Patriot Act.

11. What are some of the acts that are criminalized by recent **anti-terrorist legislation**? What are some of the constitutional objections to some of this legislation? (Criminal Law)

Some main points: It is a federal crime to harbor or conceal terrorists. It is also a crime to provide material support to terrorists and terrorist organizations. These laws are frequently challenged on the basis of void-for-vagueness and interfering with First Amendment rights of association.

12. As your department's emergency management officer, you have been directed to establish a policy and procedure to respond to **terrorist threats** in your jurisdiction. Include the roles of local, state and federal agencies in your policy and procedure.

13. Go to the websites of the DEA (www.dea.gov), the FBI (www.fbi.gov), the Department of Justice (www.usdoj.gov) and the Department of the Treasury (www.ustreas.gov) and note how the different agencies are **addressing the issue of** *terrorism*. How do their focuses differ? Be prepared to share your findings with the class.

14. Search for *USA PATRIOT Act* (2001). List specific applications of the act to law enforcement practices and explain how they might differ from conventional practices. Do you believe the phrase "extraordinary times demand extraordinary measures" justifies "bending the rules," so to speak, in the war on terrorism? In other words, do the ends justify the means? Should law enforcement be permitted to use roving wiretaps and breach privileged inmate-attorney communications in the name of national security, or is this the beginning of the end of our civil liberties? Be prepared to discuss your answers with the class.

15. Does your police department have a **counterterrorism strategy** in place? If so, what?

    Answers will vary depending on the size of the agency responsible for law enforcement in the jurisdiction in which the school is located. Students should check with their local law enforcement agencies and report their findings.

16. Do you think **a terrorist sleeper cell** could operate in your community? What signs might indicate that such a cell exists?

17. **Law Enforcement Changes:** As part of an honors project, your professor has assigned the following final exercise for your class: List and discuss ten significant changes in U.S. federal, state, and

local law enforcement as a result of the September 11, 2001 terrorism attacks on U.S. soil.

18. Before beginning your lecture, have your students write on a piece of paper a definition of terrorism in their own words. Once finished, have the students hand in the pieces of paper, and read aloud the definitions to the class. Use the class' definitions to illustrate how **definitions of terrorisms** are varied.

19. Have students discuss current **tactics of terrorists** vs. past tactics of terrorists. How have the tactics changed over time?

20. **History of Modern Terrorism:** Have students create a time line on how modern terrorism evolved. Make sure dates and prominent figures are emphasized on the timeline.

21. Is the **IRA** active in the twenty-first century? Have students research whether or not the IRA is active. Make sure students address the current targets of the IRA and the tactics that the IRA uses.

22. Have students **research a terrorist organization** (e.g. IRA, The Order). Allow students time to uncover the key players of the organization. Once the students have had time to gather information on the chosen organization, have the students diagram the organization using the pyramid model.

23. Discuss the **new types of terrorism** that emerged in the 1990s. Have students brainstorm types of terrorist organizations that could emerge in the twenty-first century.

24. Have students discuss whether or not "**leaderless resistance**" has the potential of being a successful terrorist organization. Discuss what is needed for an organization to succeed.

25. Before the lecture, have the students describe what they define as **religious terrorism**, and how it differs from other forms of terrorism. Make sure to have the students use the information they have learned from previous chapters to generate their answers.

26. Bring to class a number of **religious myths** from different religions. Read the stories to the class. Have the class divide into groups and define the sacred story in common language. After the

myth has been translated, ask the students to describe how conflict may occur due to the translation.

27. Divide the students into two groups. Assign each group a position and have them discuss the views regarding the **relation of Islam to terrorism.**

28. **Terrorist Group Funding:** Before the class, have the students explore the possible methods terrorists use to fund their organizations. Write the ideas on the board, and discuss with the class which of the methods they have chosen would be more applicable to current terrorist groups than other methods.

29. **Obstruction of Funding:** Explain that in order to prevent terrorism, the government must cut off the sources of funding. Have the students discuss possible methods as to how the governments can obstruct funding operations within terrorist organizations.

30. Discuss the opposing positions of the **narcoterrorism debate**, and have the students take a position. Once they have chosen which side of the debate to argue, have the students research drugs and terrorism, and find evidence that supports the position they have taken.

31. Have the students create a list of possible ways terrorists could use computers. After the list has been generated, discuss the importance of counterterrorism in regards to **cyberterrorism.** (Forensics and Technology)

32. **Suicide bombing** is one of the most popular terrorist tactics used today. Have the students bring print media articles to class regarding suicide bombers. Discuss the reasons as to why this tactic was used, and possible ways to reduce suicide attacks.

33. On the front board, write the effects of different **biological and chemical weapons.** Without using their books, have the students match the correct agent to the symptoms listed on the board. If desired, offer incentives to the students such as extra credit or candy.

34. Have students construct a timeline illustrating the **evolution of Osama bin Laden and al Qaeda**. Place the timeline in the front of the classroom and refer to it during your lecture.

35. Have the students discuss the differing opinions about **U.S. actions in Afghanistan and Iraq.** Make sure students are using information from outside sources and the readings, and not basing their argument purely on opinions and emotions.

36. Compare **Christianity and Muslim**. Discuss the militant factors of each religion, as well as the peaceful aspects. Have the students discuss how militant Christianity has influenced recent developments in international terrorism.

37. Discuss whether or not **Hezbollah** is a terrorist organization. Divide the class into positions, choosing a group who defends Hezbollah and a group who criticizes Hezbollah. Have the students search for information supporting their assigned arguments. After the students have their arguments prepared, have the students present the ideas in a debate format. Assign a neutral group or an outside figure to act as a judge for the debate. Instructor may offer incentives to the group who has the stronger argument.

38. The **fall of the Soviet Union** had an impact on the growth of terrorist organizations. Provide the class with information regarding the steps leading to the collapse. Using information from previous lectures, have the students discuss the political climate of the Soviet Union, and how that climate was important as far as supporting the growth of the **Jihadist movement**.

39. Have the students discuss a number of **terrorist organizations** operating throughout the world. Have the students break into groups and create an organizational chart for the different groups. Display the charts in the front of the classroom after the charts have been formatted. Using the charts, explain to the class how each organization fits under the umbrella of al Qaeda and Hezbollah.

40. Before beginning your lecture, have the students express what they already know about the **Israel-Palestinian conflict**. Ask them questions regarding the beginning of the conflict, the current state

of the conflict, and what they feel the United States could do, if anything, to help resolve the conflict.

41. Have the students make a portfolio or collage of newspaper and magazine articles that represent the **Israel-Palestinian conflict**. Have the students present their collage, identifying the groups and/or leaders that have been discussed in class and from their readings.

42. **Historical Timeline:** On the front board, or on a poster board display, draw a timeline with only dates. Have the students come up to the board one at a time, and fill in the event that corresponds with the date. Have the students discuss the event that they added to the board.

43. Have the students discuss several **terrorist organizations**. Have students break into groups, and assign each group an organization. Have the students research their assigned organization and present to the class the current state of their organization.

44. Before lecture, have the students write on a piece of paper their definition of **ethnic terrorism**, and how ethnic terrorism differs from other types of terrorism. Have the students turn in their paper. After reading the responses, have the students formulate a class definition. Also, write the differences between ethnic terrorism and other types of terrorism on the board for further discussion.

45. Show clips from the film *Bloody Sunday* (2002) to illustrate the **conflict in Ireland**. After the film, have the students discuss the conflict and their personal views on the current state of the IRA and other ethnic terrorist groups.

46. Have the students generate a list of violent groups associated with ideology. Write the list on the board, and have the students discuss which groups are terrorist groups and which are not. Explain to the class the difference between the violence associated with **ideological violence and ideological terrorism**.

47. Using some of the terrorist organizations discussed throughout the course, have the students examine the underlying theory of an assigned terrorist group. Does the assigned group use the **Marighella model** or some other type of model? Have the groups explain their findings to the rest of the class.

48. Have the students bring in print media covering **insurgent activities in Iraq**. Organize and display the insurgent activities into the three types. Have the class discuss the insurgents, and identify which actions are acts of terrorism and which are not.

49. Have the students identify **domestic terrorist groups** in the United States. Using the definitions from the chapter, have the students discuss why they defined these groups as terrorist groups.

50. Have the students print out and bring to class the **FBI's definition of terrorism**. Have the students discuss the definition and offer possible changes to make the classification of terrorist activity less confusing.

51. Before the instructor begins lecturing, have the students create their own **classification system for terrorism**. Compare the students' models to the models discussed in the chapter.

52. Have the students research the actions of **ELF, ALF, and antiabortion attacks**. Compare and contrast these movements, and discuss the potential dangers of each movement. Based on the readings, have the students discuss which type of organization they feel has the potential to become increasingly violent and generate more support.

53. Have students investigate the local law enforcement. Have them research what the police are doing to **counter terrorism**. How is information shared? After the students investigate the police, have them discuss possible techniques that would be effective against terrorism.

54. Before discussing terrorist attacks on US soil, have the students compare and contrast **Pearl Harbor and 9-11**. Discuss motive, tactics, and the effect on the American public.

55. Bring in a copy of **Title II of the Patriot Act**. Have the students read the Title, and then assign the students into two groups. Have one group argue in support of Title II, and have the other group argue in opposition of Title II. Instructor may offer incentives to the group with the stronger argument.

56. Have the students discuss the following questions: Does the criminal justice system have a role in **homeland security**? Do

criminal justice agencies want to assume this role, and do the public they serve want them to assume it? Have students use examples from outside sources (e.g., the media, their text book, the Internet) to support their position.

57. Have the students construct an organizational chart of **homeland security.** Refer to the chart when discussing Weber's ideal bureaucracy, the reality of bureaucracy, and the functions of homeland security.

58. Discuss the **bureaucratic inhibitors to homeland security.** These inhibitors are apparent in every bureaucratic organization. Have the students brainstorm possible ways to overcome the obstacles of the current bureaucratic system. Afterwards, discuss why the inhibitors continue to exist.

59. **Media Perspectives on Terrorism:** Give the students a current affair to investigate. The students are to go to various news sources (Al Jazeera, BBC, FOX, NBC, The Guardian...) to see if the story differs depending on the source. Have the students prepare a write-up of their findings.

60. Have the students bring in **media images** from U.S. new sources of terrorists or terrorist activities. Have the students discuss how terrorism is viewed, and how terrorism may be viewed differently in different parts of the world.

61. **Censorship** continues to be a wide debate among many. Have the students re-read the "censorship debates" section in the text. Separate the class into two groups, and assign each group a position to take regarding censorship. Instructor may offer incentives to the group that provides the best argument. After the debate, allow the students to express their own position on the issue of censorship.

62. Have students review the public websites of the Central Intelligence Agency (http://www.cia.gov/index.html) and the Homeland Security Department (http://www.dhs.gov/dhspublic/) for **information on terrorism** in the United States.

Ask them to provide a written response to the following questions based on their review of these sites:

a. Which group or groups do you believe represent the greatest threat to the U.S., and why? What methods would you be most concerned about them using?

b. Do the sites present different points of view as to the danger levels that various groups posed to the U.S.? If so, summarize the different perspectives as well as their sources and explain which you would consider to be the most authoritative.

63. Break the class into several groups and have the groups discuss answers to the following questions. (Criminal Investigation)

a. Which community organizations, governmental agencies, and other groups should be included in developing a community or **hometown security plan**?

b. A number of unmarried young men from the Middle East have moved into your community in recent months. What actions, if any, should be taken?

c. The Department of Homeland Security has notified you, as a member of the local police department, that a group of individuals who may be a **sleeper cell for Al-Qaeda** have been making drawings and taking pictures of a major bridge in your community.

64. Assign groups to various **terrorism events** that have occurred in the last 10 years in the United States and abroad. Key events may include the September 11, 2001 attack on the United States, the Oklahoma City Bombing, events in the Middle East, and the Unabomber. How have these events changed the United States? (Criminology)

65. Much of the discussion on **police profiling** centers on studies that have examined this practice with black and Latino citizens. In light of today's terrorist concerns and military actions, to what extent is profiling an issue for citizens from the Middle East? (Policing)

# CHAPTER 5

# COURTS

## Courts

1.  Invite a judge to class to discuss the differences between the various **state courts**.

2.  Arrange for the class to sit in on hearings in a specialty court, such as a **drug court**. (Drugs)

3.  Assign students to learn where the **court of final appeals** is located in their home states.

4.  Assign students to learn which **U.S. Court of Appeals** include their home states.

5.  Encourage students to learn about the current **U.S. Supreme Court justices**. Assign them to see how the various justices voted on particular cases.

6.  **Judicial qualifications:** Find out what kinds of qualifications are required for particular types of judges in your state. Engage students in a discussion of these qualifications. (Careers)

7.  Have students put together a list of **judicial qualifications** for the "ideal" judge. (Careers)

8.  Invite a **prosecutor** and a **defense attorney** to come to class and discuss their occupations. This is an especially effective activity if one of them is a former graduate of your program. (Careers)

9.  **Supreme Court Cases Processing:** Find a case that has been ruled on by the Supreme Court. Develop a paper on the processes and courts the case had to pass through before reaching the Supreme Court.

10. Develop a paper on legal services for the **indigent**.

11. Invite a judge to class to discuss what **pretrial services** are available and how **bail** is determined in your jurisdiction.

12. Invite a federal prosecutor to class to discuss the role of the **grand jury**.

13. Encourage student discussion of whether or not **plea-bargaining** should be abolished.

14. Invite a judge, a prosecutor and a defense attorney to class to discuss their views on **plea-bargaining**.

15. Invite a prosecutor to class to discuss his or her role the **pretrial diversion** process.

16. Develop a paper on the controversies surrounding **plea bargains**.

17. Develop a paper on the issues surrounding **preventive detention**.

18. All states have a **speedy trial statute**. Assign students to learn about this statute in their home states. This can lead to a discussion of the differences in these statutes.

19. **Televised trials:** Encourage student discussion on the issue of whether or not criminal trials should be televised.

20. If any students have ever served on a **jury** ask them to share their experiences.

21. Engage students in a discussion of **juror qualifications**. What kinds of qualifications do they think the "ideal" juror should have?

22. Arrange for the class to sit in on a **criminal trial**. Have them take note of the various kinds of **evidence** presented.

23. Arrange for students to participate in a **mock jury trial**. Occasionally, attorneys want to "try" their cases in mock trials.

24. Develop a research paper on the topic of the "**speedy trial**."

25. Develop a paper on the pros and cons of **trial broadcasts**.

26. Have students discuss which **philosophy of punishment** is closest to their own views.

27. Invite a sentencing judge to come to class and discuss the **sentencing structures** in your jurisdiction.

28. Encourage student discussion of the **three-strikes laws**. Do they think they are effective? (Criminal Law)

29. Arrange for the class to sit in on the **sentencing** phase of a criminal trial.

30. Arrange a class debate on the pros and cons of the **death penalty**.

31. Develop a research paper on **determinate versus indeterminate sentences.**

32. Encourage student discussion of sentencing circles. Are they supportive of this type of **restorative justice**? (Community Corrections and Probation)

33. Develop a paper on the principles of **restorative justice**. (Community Corrections and Probation)

34. Invite a judge to class who deals with juvenile cases. Have him or her discuss the various stages of the **juvenile justice process**. (Juvenile Justice)

35. Find out what the statutes are in your state concerning **waiver to adult court**. Discuss these with the class. How do they feel about the issue of trying juveniles as adults? At what age do they think juveniles should be tried as adults? (Juvenile Justice, Criminal Law)

36. Talk to the public defender's office or the local bar association defenders to determine how difficult it is to help suspects keep their **Fourth Amendment rights**. (Criminal Law)

37 Visit the nearest **court administrator** (judge or civilian) and discuss structure and function of the local court.

38. **State court structure:** Using library or Internet sources, chart and describe the structure and functions of your state's court system.

39. Interview and discuss the **efficiency of local trials** with a judge, prosecutor, or defender. Prepare a one-page opinion piece on conditions in your jurisdiction for class discussion.

40. How much **publicity** is there about trials in your jurisdiction? If there is a lot, what issues are discussed? If there is little, why is that?

41. Obtain a copy of the Bill of Rights and identify in it all the **due process rights**. (Criminal Law)

42. Find out in interviews with your adult neighbors how many of their **due process rights** they know. (Criminal Law)

43. What does your state or federal legislator think should be the **purpose of punishment**? After all, that person makes the laws. Look in the newspaper files at election time to see where he or she stood on these issues. If there was no issue here, why? (Punishment and Sentencing)

44. Judges are selected by varying systems. Compare and contrast the various methods of **judicial selection**. Then choose the one you would prefer to have in your jurisdiction. Please justify your opinion in a 1,500 word essay using data and cite the sources for all data used.

45. The **Adversary System of Justice** has many distinct features as does the Inquisitorial System of Justice as used in England. Compare and contrast the two systems. Focus on five issues which tend to clearly separate the two systems. Please provide a 1,500 word essay using data and cite the sources for all data used.

46. **Money and Justice:** It would seem that money significantly influences the course of justice in the United States. For example, recently a small county could not sustain a complex murder trial for lack of money. How does money affect justice? Concentrate your opinion on the three most important (in your opinion) areas of the prosecution and trial process. Please justify your opinions in a 1,500 word essay using data and cite the sources for all data used.

47 Have the students watch a television show about the criminal justice process prior to a field trip to a courthouse. Then, students should discuss in class the difference between the image of the criminal justice system as portrayed in the media and the reality of the system. This can be used to highlight the **crime control and due process models**. (Criminal Justice)

48. Students often take for granted that the criminal law process is designed in a rational manner and that the American system is the best in the world. One way to encourage students to question and analyze the components of **the criminal law process** is to require them to discuss and debate the desirability of the various steps in the process. Stage mini-debates by having pairs of students come

to the front of the class and square off in a quick pro versus con debate about the necessity and desirability of the following steps in the criminal justice process: booking, initial appearance, grand jury, arraignment, and appeal. Obviously, some students would be asked to play devil's advocate in arguing for the abolition of specific steps in the process. By staging debates, students would be required to think seriously (and persuasively) about the underlying purpose of each step in the process. Students could also be encouraged to suggest reforms for the criminal justice process and alternative steps that could be incorporated.

49. Exercise: **System Attributes**

Imagine that you are a county prosecutor. Briefly describe how the attributes of the criminal justice system (discretion, resource dependence, sequential tasks, and filtering) would affect your relationships, decisions, and actions with respect to each of the following. (Criminal Justice)

a. Police
b. Defense Attorneys
c. Trial Judges
d. News Media
e. County Commissioners

50. Exercise: **Steps in the Process**

Briefly describe what happens at each of the following steps in the justice process.

a. Booking
b. Preliminary Hearing
c. Grand Jury Proceeding
d. Arraignment
e. Trial
f. Sentencing
g. Appeal

51. Exercise: **The Insanity Defense**

Over the course of seven years, a mother has five babies and they all die during the first months of their lives. Doctors conclude that each child died from Sudden Infant Death Syndrome (SIDS) --

commonly known as "crib death" -- the unexplainable cause of death for 7,000 to 8,000 American babies each year. The woman's family doctor publishes an article about her family to show how SIDS tragically seems to run in families, perhaps for unknown genetic reasons. Years later a prosecutor notices the article and charges the woman with murdering all of her children. The woman initially confesses during police questioning but later claims that the police pressured her to confess. You are hired as her defense attorney. A psychiatrist friend of yours tells you that your client might suffer from a psychiatric condition known as "Munchausen's syndrome by proxy." You hope to use this information to consider presenting an insanity defense. (Criminal Law)

a. Search the Internet for the term "Munchausen's syndrome by proxy." What is the definition?

b. Briefly explain whether or not your client's condition can fulfill the requirements of the various tests for the insanity defense.

- M'Naughten
- Irresistible Impulse
- Durham
- Substantial Capacity
- Federal Comprehensive Crime Control Act

52. Exercise: **The Fourth Amendment and the Exclusionary Rule**

A woman called the police to her home after her daughter was severely beaten earlier in the day by the daughter's boyfriend. The daughter agreed to use her key to let the officers into the apartment where the man was sleeping. The officers did not seek to obtain either an arrest warrant or a search warrant. After the daughter unlocked the apartment door, the officers entered and found a white substance, which later proved to be cocaine, sitting on a table. They arrested the sleeping man and charged him with narcotics offenses. The defendant sought to have the drugs excluded from evidence because the officers' warrantless search was based on permission from the girlfriend who had moved out of the apartment several weeks earlier and therefore had no authority to give the officers permission to enter and search. (Policing, Criminal Law)

a. As the prosecutor, think about possible exceptions to the exclusionary rule, such as those discussed for the Fourth and Fifth Amendments, to make arguments about why the evidence should not be excluded.

b. Now, imagine that you are the judge. Decide whether the evidence obtained in the warrantless search should be excluded. Provide reasons for your decision. Consider the words of the Fourth Amendment, the purposes of the Amendment, and the potential effects on society from the rule you formulate for this case.

53. Exercise: **The Fifth and Sixth Amendments**

After arresting a suspect for burglary, police officers learned that the suspect's nickname was "Butch." A confidential informant had previously told them that someone named "Butch" was guilty of an unsolved murder in another city. The police in the other city were informed about this coincidence and they sent officers to question the suspect about the murder. Meanwhile, the suspect's sister secured the services of a lawyer to represent her brother on the burglary charge. Neither she nor the lawyer knew about the suspicions concerning the unsolved murder case. The lawyer telephoned the police station and said she would come to the station to be present if the police wished to question her client. The lawyer was told that the police would not question him until the following morning and she could come to the station at that time. Meanwhile, the police from the other city arrived and initiated the first of a series of evening questioning sessions with the suspect. The suspect was not informed that his sister had obtained the services of a lawyer to represent him. The suspect was not told that the lawyer had called the police and asked to be present during any questioning. During questioning, the suspect was informed of his Miranda rights, waived his right to be represented by counsel during questioning, and subsequently confessed to the murder. (Policing, Criminal Law)

a. If you were the defense attorney, what arguments would you make to have the confession excluded from evidence?

93

b. If you were the judge, would you permit the confession to be used in evidence? Provide reasons for your decision.

54. Have the students visit a local **courthouse** and record their experiences. Students should summarize the experience and provide thoughtful analysis of how the courthouse could function more effectively. Each student should present the research in class and then discussion and questions should follow each presentation.

55. Divide the class into small groups. Each group is a legislative committee assigned the task of proposing legislation concerning the best method for **selecting state trial judges**. Each group should consider the relative advantages and disadvantages of partisan elections, nonpartisan elections, merit selection, gubernatorial selection, and legislative selection. Students can also consider whether there are other requirements or alternative procedures that would improve the selection of judges. In considering selection methods, students should consider the following issues:

a. Should the voting public have a direct voice in the selection and removal of judges?

b. Do elected judges have sufficient independence to make proper decisions?

c. Can voters vote for judges intelligently without having a party label on the ballot to tell them about the candidates' partisan affiliations?

d. What kinds of issues should judges be permitted to discuss in judicial elections?

e. Can a merit selection process remove political considerations from the selection of judges?

f. Should trial judges be required to have any special qualifications?

g. What kinds of people would be selected for judgeships if choices were determined by governors or legislatures?

When the students later discuss the exercise in class, there may be a strong superficial attraction to the concept of merit selection.

Many students have difficulty recognizing that it is difficult for anyone to choose among a range of experienced lawyers in order to say with any precision that one lawyer is "most qualified." Moreover, scholarly research on merit selection has revealed that such processes are infused with politics as interest groups battle to gain representation on merit selection committees and appointing authorities (usually governors) tend to favor finalists who share their political values and perspectives. In addition, the public rarely has enough awareness of any specific judge's judicial performance in order to hold that judge accountable through the retention elections that normally require the citizens to approve periodically the continued tenure of a merit-selected judge.

Students may also be attracted to nonpartisan elections without recognizing that such elections often are actually guided by political parties that lurk unseen beneath the surface. Moreover, voters have difficulty distinguishing between candidates when there is no party label on the ballot to inform voters about each candidate's political inclinations.

56. Have a group of students interview a bail bondsperson and present the research before the class. This should stimulate discussion and analysis about the realities of the **bail process**.

57. Exercise: **Bail**

Imagine that you are a judge responsible for setting bail. For each of the following cases, indicate whether you would order Release on Own Recognizance (ROR), set bail at some specific amount [state the amount], or deny bail and order preventive detention. Provide brief comments that explain each decision.

a.  Jane Williams is a new assistant professor of literature at the local university. She is twenty-six years old. She has no relatives in the area and her family lives 500 miles away in the city where she went to college for the eight years it took to earn her undergraduate and graduate degrees. She is charged with fraud in obtaining $50,000 in student loans during the previous three years by lying about her income and assets on student loan application forms. Seven years earlier she pleaded guilty in her home town to a misdemeanor charge of underage drinking.

b.   Karl Schmidt is charged with attempted rape. He is accused of attacking a woman in his car while giving her a ride home from the bar where he met her. He is a twenty-two year old, rookie police officer [now suspended from the force] who has lived in the city for his entire life and has no prior record.

c.   Susan Claussen is charged with theft for ordering and eating dinner at an expensive restaurant, and then leaving without paying the bill. She has been charged with and entered guilty pleas to the offense on five previous occasions over the past three years. She has been placed on probation several times and served one thirty-day jail sentence. She is unemployed and a life-long resident of the city. She lives with her parents.

58. **Judicial Selection**: Respond to the following questions in light of the importance of judicial selection methods. Think about the implications and consequences of each selection method (Gubernatorial Appointment, Legislative Appointment, Partisan Election, Nonpartisan Election, and Merit Selection)

a.   What are the four most important qualities that we should look for in the people we select to be judges?

b.   How do we know which people possess these qualities?

c.   Which judicial selection method would provide the best means to identify and select the people who possess these qualities?

d.   What are the drawbacks to this judicial selection method?

e.   Which judicial selection method is used in the state where you live or go to school? Why do you think that this state uses this selection method instead of one of the other methods?

59. **Prosecutors** are central actors in the criminal justice process. Prosecutors must make decisions within a resource scarce environment while maintaining relationships with other actors in the system and, in many jurisdictions, with the voting public.

Tell the members of the class to imagine that they are small town prosecutors and they must make decisions about a series of cases. They may be formed into small groups or you may permit them to analyze the exercise as individual decision makers. Class members should prioritize the following cases and make decisions about how to proceed (i.e., dismiss charges, recommend bail, negotiate pleas, or prepare for an eventual trial). As prosecutors, they are confronted with the following constraints:

a. The local jail is under a court order that prohibits unconstitutional overcrowding. Thus only two people can be in the small jail within the next month because the other cells are filled with people serving short sentences.

b. The next election is only one month away and the prosecutor's opponent in closely monitoring decisions in individual cases in order to look for cases that can demonstrate that the prosecutor is not really tough on crime.

c. There are only two assistant prosecutors in this small town office who assist in processing cases.

The prosecutor must decide what to do about the following cases:

a. The twenty-year-old son of a wealthy doctor who makes contributions to the prosecutor's political campaigns has been arrested for his third drunk driving offense. The prosecutor's normal policy has been to refuse to offer attractive plea bargains to three-time offenders in order to insure that they are sentenced to at least a month in jail. The defendant's attorney has offered to have the young man make a quick guilty plea to reckless driving in exchange for a sentence of probation.

b. A drifter who hitchhiked into town has been arrested for larceny for stealing two buckets of fried chicken from a fast food restaurant. A computer check reveals that he has three prior larceny convictions and therefore could be charged under the state's "habitual offender statute" which mandates five additional years in prison be added to the sentence of incarceration for larceny. If any cash bail is set for him, he has no resources to use to obtain his release pending the outcome of his case. No counsel has yet been appointed to represent him.

c. A store clerk, who is a life-long resident of the town, has been arrested for gradually stealing $10,000 from his employer. He denies the charges. Circumstantial evidence points to this employee as the culpable individual since he was in charge of moving cash from the cash register to the store safe and he owns an expensive car that no one can believe is affordable for someone with a store clerk's wages. The clerk's attorney insists that his client will not accept a plea bargain.

d.   A college student who was visiting her parents was murdered in a wooded area while she was out jogging. A man who lived next to the woods disappeared the day that the student was reported missing. Tire marks from his truck were found near the body, but he regularly drove his truck throughout the woods. No other physical evidence linked him or any other suspect to the crime, but a computer check revealed that many years before he had served a prison sentence for manslaughter after being convicted of killing a young girl. The local newspaper has harshly criticized the police chief for not adequately investigating the crime. The police arrested the man when he returned to town after a month-long absence. The man refuses to answer any questions and the police have asked you to seek a high bail so that he cannot be released from jail while they continue to seek more evidence.

e.   A seventeen-year-old boy is arrested for shooting his father with a hunting rifle. He claims that the shooting was accidental. The father is in a coma. There are no other witnesses. The boy's mother wants him kept in jail because she does not believe that the shooting was accidental. The attorney appointed to represent the boy wants him to be released on his own recognizance pending processing of the case.

f.   A homeless man, who sleeps in alleys near the town's business district and begs for coins from passersby on Main Street, is arrested for breaking the window of a furniture store. This is the third window at a business that he has broken within the past month. Local business owners want him held in jail so that he will stop disrupting their businesses and causing property damage.

In describing these cases to the class, you may want to write descriptions on the board in outline form:

a.   Drunk driving, third offense

- son of wealthy campaign contributor
- usual procedure is to insist on jail term
- offers to plead to lesser charge for probation

b.  Larceny charge, potential habitual offender case
   - drifter who lacks connections to community
   - no resources for any cash bail

c.  Employee theft from business, $10,000
   - circumstantial evidence
   - expresses unwillingness to plea bargain

d.  Murder
   - prior record for manslaughter
   - suspicious behavior
   - lack of physical evidence
   - public
   - outcry and pressure on police

e.  Shooting, potential felonious assault
   - claims it was an accident
   - family wants him kept in jail

f.  Property damage; third time
   - homeless defendant
   - pressure from businesses to keep him off the streets

In deciding what to do and subsequently discussing these decisions, the students should identify the factors that influenced their decisions.

60. **Counsel for Indigents:** If you were given the responsibility for selecting the method of providing counsel for indigent defendants within your local courthouse, which method would you choose?

For each method listed below, state whether you would select that method and explain why or why not?

a.  Assigned Counsel

b.  Contract Counsel

c.  Public Defender

d.  Is there some other feasible alternative?

61. The students should imagine that they are the new county prosecutor and they want to eliminate **courtroom workgroups** because of a belief that the assistant prosecutors and defense attorneys have become too "cozy" in agreeing to plea bargains with light sentences. Ask the students what steps they would take to eliminate courtroom workgroups. Then discuss what might happen to case processing in the courthouse if such steps were actually taken.

62. Each student should be paired with a classmate as a prosecutor team or a defense attorney team. If there are not an equal number of prosecutor or defense attorney teams, some teams can be given three members or individuals can face off against each other as prosecutors and defense attorneys. Each team should be given the following facts and then spend several minutes deciding on a goal and strategy for **plea bargaining**. After each team has developed its strategy and assessment of the case, each prosecutor team will meet with a defense attorney team in an effort to achieve a plea bargain. After the teams have negotiated, the entire class can discuss the exercise and the different kinds of agreements that were reached.

Facts:

A seventeen-year-old male is arrested for taking a baseball bat into a convenience store, striking the clerk on the arm with the bat, and taking $200 from the store's cash register. When police officers responded to the store's silent alarm, they apprehended the young man as he walked down the street carrying a baseball bat. He claimed that he was returning home from using a batting practice machine located at a nearby miniature golf course. He was carrying $200 in cash in his pocket when arrested. The prosecutor filed charges of first degree assault (assault with a weapon) and aggravated robbery (robbery with a weapon) against the defendant.

Because the defendant recently entered a guilty plea and was awaiting sentencing for unauthorized use of a motor vehicle, if convicted, he will be regarded as a repeat offender. As a repeat offender, under the state's sentencing guidelines the defendant faced mandatory punishments of 54 months imprisonment for first degree assault and 32 months imprisonment for aggravated robbery. If convicted of both charges, a judge, upon the prosecutor's recommendation, could order the defendant to serve the prison sentences either consecutively (one after another) or concurrently (simultaneously). If the charges were reduced by the prosecutor or if a jury ultimately convicted the defendant of lesser included offenses instead of these original charges, the defendant faced potential penalties of 26 months for second degree assault and 23 months for simple robbery or 13 months for simple theft.

The convenience store's surveillance camera was not working the night of the robbery. The store clerk, a college student, is certain that he accurately identified the defendant as the robber, but the clerk was not wearing his eyeglasses at the time that the robbery occurred. The defendant was never arrested for anything prior to his recent arrest for unauthorized use of a motor vehicle. While out on bail pending sentencing on the motor vehicle charge, the defendant had been living with a local minister and continuing to attend high school. The minister posted bail for the defendant again and arranged for the defendant to enroll in a church-sponsored boarding school for troubled youths located in another state if the defendant is not imprisoned. Everyone in the state is aware that the state's prisons are overcrowded and that a federal court has ordered the state to either release some prisoners or else arrange for additional facilities to be used as prisons.

63. This exercise is designed to encourage students to think about how a prosecutor or defense attorney might employ **peremptory challenges** in an effort to obtain a favorable jury.

Divide the class into two groups. Tell one group to pretend that they are all prosecutors while the other group is to act as if they are defense attorneys. The attorneys from each side are opposing each other in a rape case in a state that uses six-member juries.

The married, twenty-six-year-old white male defendant is charged with sexually assaulting a single, twenty-one-year-old white female co-worker in his car when giving her a ride home from an office party at which both of them drank several beers.

Listed below are the profiles of the jurors remaining in the juror pool who have not been challenged for cause. After considering the brief description of each potential juror, each student should

101

write down for him- or herself the three jurors that should be excluded through the use of peremptory challenges (from the perspective of their assigned role as a prosecutor or defense attorney).

After the students have made their choices, the entire class can discuss why particular jurors were singled out for exclusion. Presumably there will be variation in the choices made by all of the students who are prosecutors as well as by all of the students who are defense attorneys.

Juror #1: white female, age 65, college graduate, retired elementary school teacher, registered Republican, married, three grown sons in their 30s, active in Methodist church.

Juror #2: African-American male, age 22, part-time college student majoring in Communication, full-time employee at office supply store, unmarried, registered Democrat, active in Baptist church.

Juror #3: white female, age 25, married, no children, college graduate, manager of fast food restaurant, registered Independent.

Juror #4: white male, age 46, married, one daughter and one son in their mid-20s, high school graduate, autoworker at large Ford plant, Vietnam War veteran, registered Democrat.

Juror #5: white female, age 31, college graduate, independent insurance agent, married, one young son, registered Republican, member of the National Rifle Association (NRA).

Juror #6: African-American female, age 38, college graduate, social worker, married, two teenage daughters, registered Democrat, active in the National Organization for Women (NOW).

Juror #7: Mexican-American female, age 45, high school graduate, legal secretary, married, two daughters and one son in their early 20s, registered Independent, active in Catholic Church.

Juror #8: white male, age 20, unmarried, unemployed high school graduate who has worked a series of low-paying jobs, lives at home with parents, registered Independent.

Juror #9: Mexican-American male, age 36, manager of bank branch, college graduate, married, one small son, registered Republican.

Juror #10: white male, age 70, high school graduate, retired postal worker, World War II veteran, registered Republican.

Juror #11: white female, age 31, attended but did not complete college, married, not currently employed outside of the home, married, three daughters in elementary school, registered Democrat.

Juror #12: white male, age 42, high school graduate, auto mechanic, married, two sons in junior high school, registered Republican, volunteer assistant football coach at high school.

During the class discussion, students should consider how they think specific demographic factors (i.e., gender, race, age, occupation, education, political party affiliation, parenthood) are likely to affect a juror's view about crime in general and about rape in particular. In addition, how might these jurors view the alleged rape situation, especially if the defendant claims that the alleged victim consented? Would any particular demographic groups blame the woman for drinking and then getting into a car alone with a man? Fundamentally, do we really have any way of knowing whether these individual jurors have any of the attitudes or biases that we attribute to their demographic groups? Are lawyers really just applying their own stereotypes and biases about groups of people in deciding how to use peremptory challenges? Do peremptory challenges, as applied by the students in the class, skew the jury's composition by disproportionately eliminating any group (e.g., women, minority group members)? Would the jury system be fairer if peremptory challenges were not permitted?

After the discussion, have the prosecutors and defense attorneys each vote on the three that should be excluded. They will then exclude anywhere from three jurors (in the unlikely event that the prosecutors and defense attorneys vote to exclude the same three jurors) to six jurors (if they each vote to exclude completely different jurors).

Now consider what kinds of strategies and arguments each side would use to persuade the remaining jurors [assume that there is a six-member jury, but that any remaining jurors would be alternates who would hear the evidence without knowing which six will actually be asked to deliberate at the end of the trial].

64. Have the students research a criminal case that has recently been decided against a defendant in the court system. This could be a high-profile case or a local case of interest. Students should prepare **an appeal** from the perspective of the criminal defendant in the criminal case. Why should this case decision be reviewed or overturned?

65. **Courtroom Workgroup:** A newly elected prosecutor has hired you as a consultant. She wants to know whether she should assign assistant prosecutors to single courtrooms to handle all cases before a specific judge or, alternatively, rotate assistant prosecutors to different courtrooms and other assignments every week. She says, "I've heard that these 'courtroom workgroups,' whatever they are, form if you keep assistant prosecutors in one courtroom. What should I do?"

    a. Define the concept of "courtroom workgroup."

    b. Describe how courtrooms will work if an assistant prosecutor is permanently assigned to one courtroom. What are the consequences?

    c. How will courtrooms work if assistant prosecutors are rotated? What are the consequences?

    d. Which approach do you recommend? Why?

66. **Plea Bargaining:** Imagine that you are the prosecutor who has been responsible for investigating and prosecuting the case of a suspected serial killer. Over the span of a few years, eight hunters, fishermen, and joggers have been found dead in isolated areas of a three-county rural area. Each one had been shot by a sniper from a great distance. Two bits of evidence led you to arrest a suspect. First, among the many tips you received about possible suspects, one informant described the employee of a nearby city water department who owned many guns and frequently drove out into the country to shoot at random animals he encountered, including

104

farmers' cows and pet dogs. Second, you knew that one of the victims was shot with a rifle that was made in Sweden and was not commonly available in local gun stores.

You learned from a second informant that the city employee sold one of these unusual Swedish rifles to another gun enthusiast shortly after the time that a hunter was killed by a shot from such a rifle. You located the gun and ballistics tests indicated a high probability that it was the weapon used in that particular murder. You charged the suspect with five of the eight murders and you scrambled to find evidence to link him with these and the remaining three murders. You have spoken publicly about seeking the death penalty. Now, after months of heavy publicity about the case, you announce that the defendant will plead guilty to one count of murder and be sentenced to life in prison. (Based on a real case in Canton, Ohio).

When giving a guest lecture in a criminal justice course at a nearby university, a student asks you to explain how the plea bargain in this case can be viewed as a "good" or "fair" result in light of the number of victims and the fact that you could have pursued the death penalty. Whether or not you personally agree with the plea bargain, in your role as the prosecutor, how would you explain the benefits of the plea bargain with respect to various interested actors and constituents listed below?

Briefly explain if and how the plea bargain benefits the:

a. Prosecutor
b. Judge
c. Court System
d. Defense Attorney
e. Defendant
f. Society
g. Victim's Families

67. **Jury Selection**: Imagine that a thirty-year-old African-American woman is facing trial for the murder of her Hispanic husband. He was shot while standing in the doorway of the house soon after he returned home from work. There are no eyewitnesses. The murder weapon had the wife's fingerprints on it. On the advice of her lawyer, she never answered any questions from the police. Several

defense witnesses will testify that the deceased husband used to beat his wife frequently.

    a. If you are the prosecutor in this case, what is the demographic profile of your ideal juror? (e.g., age, race, education, occupation, gender, political party affiliation, religion, etc.) Why?

    b. If you are the defense attorney in this case, what is the demographic profile of your ideal juror? Why?

    c. If you were the prosecutor, what questions would you want to ask the potential jurors during voir dire? Why?

    d. If you were the defense attorney, what questions would you want to ask the potential jurors during voir dire?

68. **Court Jurisdiction:** Assign students the task of finding out in what court they would be tried if they contested a speeding ticket, committed a misdemeanor, or committed a felony.

Possible discussion points: This answer will vary by jurisdiction. The speeding ticket will usually be in a municipal, traffic or Justice of the Peace Court. Depending on the seriousness of the misdemeanor, it will be handled in a municipal, Justice of the Peace, or some form of county court. Felonies are tried in the trial court of general jurisdiction.

69. **Conflict within the system:** Why is there sometimes conflict and tension between police, prosecutors and corrections? Why is there often tension and conflict between state, federal and local authorities? What are some of the costs of this tension and conflict? Without making major changes in the system, what could be done to lessen this tension and conflict?

Possible discussion points: Agencies compete for funds and favorable publicity. To defend themselves, they may criticize other agencies. Personnel in agencies may have different political philosophies. The costs of this are monetary costs, delays, lack of coordination, cases falling between the cracks and guilty people being acquitted.

70. **Court decisions:** Take your class on a field trip to a local municipal, district or similar typically misdemeanor court (for

arraignment and sentencing) and which also has felony jurisdiction for first appearance and/or preliminary hearing. After watching at least two hours of release and sentencing decisions, hold a discussion in class to debate the justifications for decisions witnessed. Invite the judge to comment to the class about the factors in making such decisions. (Punishment and Sentencing)

71. Divide your class into small groups. Give each group a set of brief vignettes – cases with brief facts alleging a misdemeanor crime, and giving information about the defendant (job, married, age, criminal history, etc.). Require each participant in the group to play a role – judge, defense attorney, prosecutor, and probation officer (for evaluation and recommendation – you might also employ a supervisor to sign off on the recommendation). Have them make written recommendations for the pre-trial status of each defendant. Require the judge to make a ruling. After all have been completed, debate in class by comparing the **group process decisions**, requiring each judge to justify their position and permitting other role players to argue with or support the ruling.

72. **Due process:** In the American criminal justice system, safeguards like the presumption of innocence, rights and due process are in place to protect our individual freedoms and to prevent putting an innocent person in prison. However, the downside is that some of the guilty go free. Is this a good system? Does it give criminals too many protections? How could the system be changed?

Possible discussion points: Perhaps not a good system, but the best system we've got. Do the guilty actually go free or just serve short sentences? Is today's justice system in line with the spirit of the Founding Fathers' ideas? Criminals are citizens too.

73. Explain why **civil remedies** may be used to combat criminal acts. Be sure to provide examples.

Some main points: It has proven somewhat cheaper and easier to go after criminal acts like drugs, etc. in civil court because of the lower burden of proof and also because it hits defendants where it counts, in their pocketbooks. Civil actions for criminal actions have also given victims a chance for retribution. Asset forfeiture is very popular and effective, sometimes too effective in punishing criminal acts.

107

74. Recently captured terrorists have become classified as military non-combatants instead of prisoners of war and are thus being tried in **secret military courts**. As a controversial topic, should these prisoners be tried in secret in the name of national security, should they be tried in regular courts, or should the U.S. even have jurisdiction over these prisoners in lieu of some kind of international court? (Terrorism and Homeland Security)

Possible discussion points: With respect to national security, is the U.S. a vigilante? Do defendants truly meet the definition of soldier or enemy and thus become subject to the Geneva Convention?

75. While the idea of a unified court system has somewhat given way to efficiency and specialty courts, what are the pros and cons of having a **unified court system**? Would such a system become a source of tension between lower and higher courts? Why did it never come to widespread fruition?

Possible discussion points: While a unified system would increase uniformity and efficiency, it would take away the ability of local jurisdictions to adapt to their individual needs. If such a system were implemented, it would create much tension between the lower and higher courts and would take a long time to be accepted. In areas where court unification did not come to fruition, it is likely due to the fact that such courts adapted to meet their needs, while others were debating the pros and cons of unification.

76. What are the five essential elements of **therapeutic jurisprudence**? Be sure to provide an example of each. What is your opinion on such an approach to crime? Be sure to explain your position.

Some main points: The five essential elements of therapeutic jurisprudence are intermediate intervention, nonadversarial adjudication, hands-on judicial involvement, treatment programs with clear rules and structured goals, and a team approach. Courts such as drug courts and other specialty courts would use this rehabilitative philosophy.

77. Although the **prosecutor** is usually the most powerful member of the courtroom work group, most people probably can't name the district or county or state's attorney for their locale. Why is this?

Shouldn't such a powerful official be better known and more accountable?

Possible discussion points: Most people are fairly apathetic about politics in general, and probably even more so about local politics. It is said, the voters get the quality of officials they deserve.

78. As our judiciary system was founded on the **adversarial model**, is true justice still being administered in the light of **courtroom work groups** and **assembly line justice**? Is this a good thing or bad thing?

Possible discussion points: If the basis of courtroom work groups and assembly-line justice is improving efficiency, saving money, and moving cases, is this fair to the defendants and their rights? Does it still amply protect defendants' rights? How great is the difference between the true adversarial model and today's more cooperative reality?

79. In general, "justice delayed is justice denied." Explain the meaning of this phrase and how it affects defendants and the courtroom workgroup. Is **delay** always harmful to the interest of everyone involved? What steps have courts and legislatures taken to deal with the problem of delay? Have these steps been effective? Be sure to provide examples.

Some main points: This old adage embodies the idea of swift and certain punishment. Not only does court delay affect defendants, it also affects the victims, the state, and the system itself. While the U.S. Constitution and thirty-five state constitutions have guarantees for speedy trials, all states have some kind of speedy trial law. The Speedy Trial Act of 1974 (amended 1979) was enacted by Congress to specify the time standards for two primary stages of the federal court process. However, certain procedures, such as hearings on pretrial motions and the mental competency of the defendant are considered excludable time. While the federal speedy trial law was enacted to protect the interests of society, the state laws are generally oriented toward protecting defendants.

Because most speedy trial laws were enacted with little regard for the sources of court delay and provide few additional resources, speedy trial laws have, for the most part, proven ineffective.

Furthermore, compliance with such laws has only been possible through the delaying of civil cases. However, federal speedy trial laws have proven to be quite effective. On average, in 1970 it took seven months for a criminal case to reach a disposition. In 1980, cases were disposed of in less than three months.

80. Do prosecuting attorneys have too much power? If so, what might be some possible solutions to curbing this potential for overzealous prosecutions?

Possible discussion points: What are the sources of **prosecutorial power**? Is centralization or other forms of checks effective?

81. Explain why the **prosecutor** is the most powerful member of the courtroom work group. Be sure to provide examples.

Some main points: Responses should include discretion, limited supervision, the control of information, and the phenomenon of a prosecutor's duties bridging all phases of the criminal justice process.

82. Are **indigent defendants** at a disadvantage by being represented by court appointed attorneys compared to privately retained attorneys?

Possible discussion points: Studies have been mixed. Consider the breakdown of the attorney-client relationship and defendants' view of attorneys: "No, I had a public defender."

83. Is it fair that the **defense attorney** is the weakest member of the courtroom work group as compared to the prosecutor who is the most powerful? What slant does this give to the justice system?

Possible discussion points: Does this put the defendant at a marked disadvantage? Does it increase the ease and likelihood for railroading innocent but disliked defendants? Does this disparity serve the greater good of society? As the burden of proof rests on the prosecution, does this even things out?

84. **Client problems:** Discuss some of the problems attorneys have with indigent clients and criminal defendants in general. Be sure to provide examples.

Some main points: Distrust, hostility, lack of cooperation, deception, dishonesty, unwillingness to accept advice, obtaining clients, and a defendant's ability to pay.

85. **Judicial power:** Contrary to popular belief, judges share power amongst the courtroom work group. Does this phenomenon stand contrary to the formal powers granted judges and their status as fair and impartial arbiters? Should judges retain their formal powers?

    Possible discussion points: Should prosecutors wield the most power of the courtroom work group? Do judges sacrifice effectiveness by sharing power with the courtroom work group? How would caseloads and the workings of the courtroom change if judges retained all of their formal powers?

86. Which of the **judicial selection methods** is the most effective? Explain and discuss.

    Possible discussion points: What type of judges does each method result in? Which method results in the best-qualified candidates? What role do politics play? What has research found?

87. Discuss the role of politics in **judicial selection and patronage**. Should and/or can politics be removed from judicial selection? Explain your position on this issue.

    Some main points: Politics obviously play heavily into each judicial selection method, but differ in form. While merit selection was supposed to take the politics out of judicial selection, it merely changed the form of politics by giving lawyers more power in judicial selection. Judges often reflect the politics of those who elect or appoint them. Furthermore, the unique powers granted to judges and the opportunity for patronage ensures the presence of politics. Many judges owe their positions to political patronage, as federal judges are likely to have been politically active in the campaigns of their appointers.

88. Discuss the characteristics of **the traditional American judge**. How might these characteristics be expected to influence their decisions?

Some main points: The traditional American judge was and continues to be a white, Protestant male, from an upper middle class background, with an above average education. Furthermore, judges are likely to have been involved in politics and represent the political ideology of their constituents or appointers. However, since the Carter administration, a growing number of women and minorities have become judges.

89. Discuss the need to balance **judicial independence and judicial accountability**. Be sure to provide examples. (Ethics)

Some main points: The rationale for judicial independence is to protect judges and the judiciary from outside control and from fallout from unpopular decisions. However, procedures must also be in place to discipline or remove errant judges, as corrupt or wayward judges deface judicial integrity and the public's confidence in the judiciary. Therefore, a delicate balance must be struck in establishing procedures and systems to protect both the judiciary and the public.

90. Briefly discuss the characteristics of the typical **felony defendant**. How do those characteristics differ from those of the typical **courtroom workgroup** members? What might be the consequences of the divergence in characteristics between the defendant and workgroup members?

Some main points: Typical felony defendants are generally younger, overwhelmingly male, less likely to be married, often come from broken homes, likely unemployed, and disproportionately members of the lower class (poor) and racial minorities. Workgroup members tend to be white, older, more educated and more affluent. The differences may lead to unfair prejudices or stereotypes of defendants.

91. Discuss some of the hardships and frustrations that **victims** endure in bringing their assailants to justice. Be sure to provide examples.

Some main points: Trial delays result in frequent travel and wasted time, long waits in uncomfortable surroundings, and lost wages for time spent in court. Victims also may face retaliation and frustrations with a system that is far different than the imagined adversarial system. In their witness capacity, victims often face intensive cross-examination, leaving them feeling as if they had been put on trial instead of the defendant.

92. Do **grand juries** violate the Constitutional rights of witnesses and defendants? Does the prosecutor have too much power in "advising" the grand jury?

Possible discussion points: Diminished rights of witnesses and defendants; grand jury reform; *U.S. v. Williams.*

93. With continuously rising caseloads, is **case attrition** a problem or simply a fact of life? What can be done to lessen case attrition?

Possible discussion points: The courtroom workgroup devotes its limited resources to serious offenses. Three factors of discretion: legal judgments, policy priorities, and personal standards of justice. Also consider quality of arrests and evidentiary strength.

94. Define, discuss, compare and contrast **trial (petit) and grand juries**.

Some main points: Grand juries are vastly different from traditional juries. Grand juries generally are made up of more members and are impaneled for a set period of time, usually three months. Grand jury proceedings are also held in secret to protect those who are merely under investigation and a simple majority is all that is needed to hand down an indictment. Furthermore, the rights of both suspects and witnesses are severely diminished. Witnesses have no right to counsel, nor do suspects have the right to present their side of the facts. Generally, grand juries have served as a rubber stamp for prosecutors.

95. **Bail bondsmen** in some states have been replaced by the courts. Does this idea have merit? Should this for profit influence be taken out of the judiciary system?

Possible discussion points: Difficulty of government in apprehending bail jumpers, strong bail enforcement lobbying, pretrial service programs.

96. What role does **pretrial detention** play in the legal processing of defendants and in maintaining the plea-bargaining system? Should it play such a role?

Possible discussion points: Pretrial jail versus pretrial release effects on case disposition; pretrial detention effects/ encouragement on plea-bargaining. Does pretrial detention create a stronger impression of implied guilt?

97. Interview a judge or prosecuting attorney (or ask them to make a class presentation). Find out what their attitude is toward **plea bargaining.**

Possible discussion points: Most judges and prosecutors will admit that plea bargaining is appropriate in the right type of case; for instance, to save a rape or child abuse victim from having to testify.

98. In many American courts for years, **plea bargaining** was officially taboo. However, it was carried on and everyone involved denied that it existed. Although the defendant, defense attorney, prosecutor, and probably the judge knew there was a bargain, its existence was denied on the record. What does this practice say about the quality and ethics of the lawyers involved? (Ethics)

Some main points: We expect courts to exemplify the highest ideals of truth, honor and justice, and yet they dishonored those ideals. It is no wonder that many people are cynical or distrustful about the criminal justice system.

99. Discuss the caseload hypothesis and other **explanations for plea bargaining**. Which theory do you think is the best explanation? Be sure to explain your position.

Some main points: The common explanation for plea bargaining is that the courts have too many cases. It was argued that although this explanation contains some truth, it obscures too many important facets of what the courts do and why they do it. But the caseload hypothesis cannot explain why plea bargaining is as prevalent in courts with relatively few cases as it is in courts with heavy caseloads. Plea bargaining is best understood not as a response to large caseloads (caseload hypothesis), but as an adaptation to the realities of the types of cases requiring disposition. In most cases, there is little question about the defendant's legal guilt. A trial is a costly and sometimes risky method of establishing that guilt, and it cannot wrestle with the

114

pressing issue of what sentence to impose. Through plea bargaining, courthouse officials are able to individualize justice. In many instances, it is neither necessary nor desirable that every defendant have a trial.

100. **Types of pleas:** Discuss, define, compare and contrast an Alford plea, a *nolo contendere* plea and a plea on the nose. Be sure to provide examples of each.

Some main points: Alford plea – guilty plea by defendant professing innocence (judge may accept if there is a factual basis for the plea); *nolo contendere* – no contest plea, criminal equivalent of not guilty, except that it cannot be used against the defendant in a civil case: plea on the nose – pleading to the original charge.

101. **Fair trial:** After the police officers charged with beating Rodney King were acquitted in state court, there was massive, violent, destructive rioting in Los Angeles. The officers were tried again in federal court and convicted. Given the pressure these jurors were under to convict, did the officers really get a fair trial?

Possible discussion points: Think about if you were a federal court juror. Would you want to have to feel responsible for more riots and deaths if you came back with an acquittal? Would you fear retribution by King's supporters?

102. What are three options a trial judge has available to deal with **prejudicial publicity** occurring before or during the trial?

Some main points: Judge has at least three options:

a.  Gag order prohibiting those involved from providing information to media

b.  Move trial to another location (change of venue)

c.  Sequester (isolate) jury and keep them together.

103. Discuss the role of *voir dire* **and challenges in jury selection.** Be sure to provide examples.

Some main points: The potential jurors will be questioned about their knowledge of the case, ability to be fair etc. This process is called voir dire. During *voir dire*, both attorneys will attempt to educate the jury on points favorable to their side. Potential jurors who cannot be fair can be stricken by challenges for cause. In addition, both sides have a limited number of peremptory challenges that can be used to eliminate potential jurors without providing a reason.

104. Discuss the role of the **Fifth and Sixth Amendments** with regard to witnesses and the defendant testifying. Be sure to provide examples.

Some main points: Each witness will be subjected to cross-examination by the opponent of the party that called them. The Sixth Amendment gives defendants the right to confront opposing witnesses. The Fifth Amendment privilege against self-incrimination gives the defendant the right not to testify if he or she so decides. However, a defendant who testifies can be cross-examined like any other witness. Each witness will be subjected to cross-examination by the opponent of the party that called them. The Sixth Amendment gives defendants the right to confront opposing witnesses.

105. Interview a criminal court judge or ask such a judge to make a presentation to the class about **sentencing, prison overcrowding**, etc. (Punishment and Sentencing)

Possible discussion points: Many judges will say that sentencing is one of the toughest parts of the job. Some may welcome the limitation of their discretion. However, most judges will probably be unhappy if their discretion is severely limited. Federal judges have been complaining about the sentencing guidelines for years.

106. How many people can name all nine **Justices on the U.S. Supreme Court**? How many people can name the Chief Justice (or any of the Justices) on their state Supreme Court? Most can name few or none. What does this indicate about **the public and the judiciary**?

Some discussion points: In states where appellate judges are elected, there is little excuse for not knowing some of the individuals. When most people go to the polls they are not really

116

concerned that much about judicial elections. Does public apathy and ignorance result in poor quality appellate judges?

107. Discuss, define, compare and contrast *en banc* **and panel decisions**.

Some main points: In intermediate appellate courts, decisions are usually made by rotating three-judge panels. However, in important cases all judges may participate (*en banc* hearing). Courts of last resort usually make decision *en banc* only.

108. Although it annually decides only around 100 cases, the **U.S. Supreme Court** is an extremely important institution in **national criminal justice policy**. Explain why this is so. Be sure to provide examples and discuss the trends of the Warren, Burger and Rehnquist Courts.

Some main points: Because it has the final say on the meaning of the Constitution, which is the supreme law of the land, the U.S. Supreme Court has been extremely important in shaping criminal justice policy. The liberal Warren Court expanded civil rights and the rights of defendants. The moderate Burger Court did not create the expected conservative counter-revolution. The current Supreme Court, the Rehnquist Court has been generally conservative, but has issued a number of important liberal decisions.

109. What is the name of the **trial court of limited jurisdiction** in your area? What is its jurisdiction? If you have had an opportunity to visit this court (as party, witness or visitor), what is your impression?

Possible discussion points: The name of the court will vary from state to state and perhaps even between some counties. Typical jurisdiction is traffic offenses, minor misdemeanors and ordinance violations. Procedures are typically informal.

110. Are there any **ADR or mediation programs** available in your community? Have you had any experience with them? If so, what is your impression?

Possible discussion points: Use of ADR and mediation programs varies widely from state to state and even community to community. In some areas, the Better Business Bureau provides mediation for disputes between its members and consumers.

111. Does the convenient, quick and relatively inexpensive access to **Justice of the Peace and Small Claims courts** justify the assembly-line procedures and questionable qualifications of the judges?

    Possible discussion points: If we don't have such courts, judges and access will allow small disputes to simmer and eventually result in violent resolution. Can society afford the costs of lawyer judges and full hearings? Will taxpayers be willing to pay the extra costs?

112. What are **lower courts** doing to try to work more closely with the communities they serve?

    Some main points: Lower courts in many states are attempting to work more closely with the local community to find non-judicial solutions to disputes. There are a number of types of Alternative Dispute Resolution (ADR) programs which try to provide less adversarial means of settling disputes. Some communities have set up community dispute settlement centers or community courts to try to use mediation to solve problems.

113. What are the maximum and minimum ages for **juvenile court jurisdiction** for delinquent acts in the state where you reside or attend college? Do you think these ages are too high or too low? What services does your state provide for children who commit crimes while under the minimum age of juvenile court jurisdiction? (Juvenile Justice)

    Possible discussion points: Most states do not provide juvenile court jurisdiction for those who reach eighteen. In Texas, juvenile court jurisdiction is not available for those who are seventeen. If the child is below juvenile court jurisdiction, the primary options are mental health, or some form of neglect/dependency proceeding.

114. What social trends will likely have an impact on juvenile crime and **juvenile courts** in the next few decades? How will the system respond to these changes? (Juvenile Justice)

118

Possible discussion points: Demographic changes such as the number of people in the crime-prone teen years will be important. As senior citizens become an increasing proportion of the population, they will compete with the children of the poor for government assistance.

115. Strict liability crimes have no *mens rea* element and thus permit punishment of those who may be blameless or who committed the crime by truly unavoidable accidents. What are pros and cons of **strict liability crimes**?

Possible discussion points: These crimes are controversial because they can punish persons who had no mental fault. A person could be punished for an accident. On the other hand, it is argued that certain types of crimes involve such important governmental interests and would be too difficult to enforce if a *mens rea* element was required. Strict liability crimes are always minor crimes that are rarely, if ever, punished by imprisonment.

116. **Proof:** What does the prosecution have to prove with regard to causation to get a conviction?

117. What are **intervening causes** and how do they affect a defendant's responsibility? Be sure to provide examples. (Criminal Law)

Some main points: If a crime has a harm or result element, the prosecution must prove that the defendant caused the harm beyond a reasonable doubt. The prosecution must prove that the defendant's acts were both (1) the cause in fact (but for cause) and (2) the proximate or legal cause. Cause in fact is an empirical or factual issue. Proximate or legal cause involves the question of whether it is fair or just to make the defendant responsible for a harm that occurred in an unusual fashion. For instance, sometimes a defendant will do an act and start a chain of events in motion, but some other event will occur after the defendant's act and contribute to causation of the harm. In general, if this intervening cause was normal and foreseeable, the defendant will not be relieved of liability for the harm.

118. In the jurisdiction where you live or go to college, what is the age at which persons are deemed to be adults and thus are tried in adult

court rather than **juvenile court**? Is this age too low or too high? Do juveniles take advantage of the system? (Juvenile Justice)

Some Discussion Points: Juveniles are probably less deterrable and more rehabilitatable than most adults. This would seem to indicate that juvenile court would be better for them and society. In Texas, persons are not eligible for juvenile court for any crime committed after they turn seventeen.

119. Does the common law approach to rape and its prosecution clearly reflect the reality of a male-dominated society where women are seen as property and untrustworthy? Have today's **rape laws** better reflected the interests and growing power of women in society?

Some discussion points: At common law, rape victims were treated with suspicion and there were a number of legal devices that help males get acquittals. A man could not rape his wife. Was this because she was his property and he had a right to sex anytime he wanted it? Reforms in rape law have paralleled the women's liberation movement.

120. Have students visit the portion of the website of the American Bar Association (ABA) that lists **ABA standards for the prosecution of cases.**

http://www.abanet.org/crimjust/standards/pfunc_toc.html

After they have reviewed these standards, ask them to respond in written form to the following questions: (Victimization, Criminal Investigation)

a. What are the ABA standards for an extrajudicial statement?

b. Is a prosecutor's office expected to offer legal advice to a law enforcement agency concerning criminal matters?

c. What is the ABA standard for relationships with victims and witnesses by the prosecutor?

121. **Court experience:** Have the students visit the local courts. Discuss their preconceived notions of court and their actual experience.

122. **Juries:** Divide the students into groups of 12. Provide each group with the same information concerning a criminal case. Ask the

students to come to a consensus as to the guilt or innocence of the offender and an appropriate penalty that may be required. Then, ask the students to present their findings to the class and compare across the final decisions.

123. Divide the students into two groups. Have one develop an argument in support of the **death penalty** and have the other develop an argument against the death penalty. Discuss which side is able to make the stronger case. How does one's own position on this topic impact his or her evaluation of the debate? (Punishment and Sentencing)

124. Exercise: **Teaching Plea Bargaining** with Deal or No Deal

To teach students the dynamics of plea bargaining, have them play a variation on the recent game show, Deal or No Deal. In the TV version, the player chooses one of 26 brief cases containing monetary amounts from 1 cent to 1 million dollars. The player's goal is to deal for the highest amount of money possible.

In the plea bargaining version, the player's goal is to deal for the lowest court penalty. The 26 brief cases in this version range from acquittal to the death penalty. To construct the game, use 26 manila folders to represent the closed brief cases. Write the number on the front of each folder, from 1 to 26. In PowerPoint, create 26 slides with penalties ranging from acquittal to the death penalty. Be sure to include fines, restitution, probation, intermediate sanctions, various amounts of prison time, life with parole, life without parole, and finally the death penalty. Whatever 26 penalties you choose to use, try to determine 26 penalties ranging from least serious (acquittal) to most serious (death penalty).

You will write this list of penalties in order on your chalkboard or white board. Print out the PowerPoint slides. Shuffle the 26 slides so they are in random order. Place them in the 26 file folders. Place them on a large table in the classroom from 1 to 26.

Select students to play the game...

a. the player
b. the dealer
c. the banker

d.   three supporters for the player

e.   the folder opener

How to Play the Game: It helps to watch the TV version to understand the rules.

a.   Have the player select his/her folder to keep. Set it aside. Be sure the folders are not so thin or in view of the student which causes the student to be able to see the penalties.

b.   The student draws 6 files, one at a time. The instructor marks them off the list on the board. The goal is to get rid of the more severe penalties. The goal is to retain the lowest penalty or to at least deal for the least severe penalty remaining.

c.   After the first six selections, the banker reviews the list to determine his/her first offer (deal). The offer (deal) is written on the board. The deal is determined by the banker to be as severe as possible taking into account which penalties the player has been able to remove. For example, if the death penalty is removed then the deal has to be less serious because the death penalty is no longer something the player has to fear. If the acquittal is removed, then the deal can be more severe since the player definitely does not have the acquittal in his/her original file. The player looks at the deal and the dealer asks the question: Deal or no deal? The player can take the deal or proceed with selections, taking the risk that the next offer (deal) may not be as good as the previous one.

d.   If the player chooses no deal, then the player selects 5 files, one at a time, with the folder opener opening each file for all to see. After the 5 files, the banker offers again and the dealer offers the deal. If the player refuses the deal, the player chooses 4 files, the offer is made, then the player chooses one by one, with a deal offer after each selection. The goal is to get out with the least severe penalty possible.

e.   The mission of the game is to teach the students that the goal of the banker (prosecutor) is to give the most severe penalty possible and the goal of the player (offender) and the supporters (defense attorneys) is to deal for the least severe penalty possible.

f. Play the game multiple times over several class periods to demonstrate how random the outcomes are. It takes 20-30 minutes to play a good round.

125. Invite a local prosecutor to address the class regarding factors used in his or her office when making **charge and plea bargaining decisions**. (Race)

126. Tell your students they are the presiding judge hearing first appearance bail applications. From your local prosecutor, obtain redacted copies of genuine arrest reports used to present the state's case at **initial appearances**. Present each case and ask the students how they would rule regarding bail for the defendant. Have them explain their reasoning. (Race)

127. Invite a local county court administrator to address the class regarding the **jury pool selection** process used in your county and the types of problems encountered. (Race)

128. Moderate an in-class debate between a team of students presenting Professor Paul Butler's views on **racially based jury nullification**, and a second team presenting author Randall Kennedy's opposing views. (Race)

129. Invite a local juvenile court judge to address your class regarding factors he or she considers when making a decision to **waive jurisdiction of a juvenile offender** to criminal court. (Race)

130. Have a juvenile court lawyer visit the class to take about **juvenile rights**. (Juvenile Justice)

131. Explain the difference between **community courts** and traditional courts. Community courts differ in the kinds of problems they have been designed to address.

132. Have the students visit the **juvenile court** in your jurisdiction. Have them interview the juvenile court judge, prosecutor, or a defense attorney who does a lot of work in juvenile court. Have them write a report on how the juvenile justice system functions in your locality. (Juvenile Justice)

## Criminal Law

1.  Invite a judge to come to class to discuss the differences between **criminal law** and **civil law**. (Punishment and Sentencing)

2.  Assign students to look up various crimes for your state and learn whether they are **felonies** or **misdemeanors**. You could then assign them to look up some of these crimes in other states to determine whether they have the same status.

3.  Prior to discussing **the insanity defense**, have students discuss their perception of it. Encourage a discussion of whether they think it is easy to claim the insanity defense. (Punishment and Sentencing)

4.  Invite a judge to class to discuss the different types of **criminal defenses** discussed in the text. (Punishment and Sentencing)

5.  Develop a research paper on the use of the **insanity defense**, using particular cases to illustrate the use of the different tests of insanity. (Punishment and Sentencing)

6.  Develop a research paper on the various **excuse defenses** discussed in the text. (Punishment and Sentencing)

7.  Develop a research paper on the evolution of **common law**.

8.  Invite both a judge and a police officer to come to class to discuss the impact of the **exclusionary rule** on policing. (Policing)

9.  Encourage student discussion of the **three-strikes laws**. Do they think they are effective? (Courts)

10.  Encourage a discussion focusing on **prisoners' rights**. Do students think that prisoners have too many rights? (Incarceration and Prison Society)

11.  Select two **prisoners' rights** and write a paper on these rights. (Incarceration and Prison Society)

12.  Find out what the statutes are in your state concerning **waiver to adult court**. Discuss these with the class. How do they feel about the issue of trying juveniles as adults? At what age do they think juveniles should be tried as adults? (Juvenile Justice, Courts)

13. Talk with a criminal attorney to learn how he or she perceives the **adequacy of the criminal law** to deal with problems today. What does this attorney think should be changed, if anything?

14. Find the most complete selection of **law books** you can that concern your state's criminal law. Where are they? How accessible are they?

15. Access the *Federal Register* and read about current changes in the law of the United States.

16. Contact an attorney through his or her website and arrange an interview about **due process rights** and their implementation as the attorney sees the matter.

17. Talk to the public defender's office or the local bar association defenders to determine how difficult it is to help suspects keep their **Fourth Amendment rights**. (Courts)

18. Research five recent news reports of violations of persons' **Fourth Amendment rights**. Compare and contrast. Describe the cases. Why were the rights violated?

19. Obtain a copy of the Bill of Rights and identify in it all the **due process rights**. (Courts)

20. Find out in interviews with your adult neighbors how many of their **due process rights** they know. (Courts)

21. Discuss the chapter material with an attorney who practices **juvenile law**. Does the interviewee accept the system as it is? Are there suggestions for improvement? What are the problems? (Juvenile Justice)

22. From the beginning of the nation, we have argued about how punitive we can be with children. The **ages of responsibility** are constantly adjusted to reflect the times and the juvenile court has been implemented. Still the debate continues. How much responsibility are we going to attribute to children of what age? (You know there are "adults" who are very irresponsible.) Focusing solely on responsibility, please justify your opinion in a 1,500 word essay using data and cite the sources for all data used. (Juvenile Justice)

23. Exercise: **The Insanity Defense**

Over the course of seven years, a mother has five babies and they all die during the first months of their lives. Doctors conclude that each child died from Sudden Infant Death Syndrome (SIDS) -- commonly known as "crib death" -- the unexplainable cause of death for 7,000 to 8,000 American babies each year. The woman's family doctor publishes an article about her family to show how SIDS tragically seems to run in families, perhaps for unknown genetic reasons. Years later a prosecutor notices the article and charges the woman with murdering all of her children. The woman initially confesses during police questioning but later claims that the police pressured her to confess. You are hired as her defense attorney. A psychiatrist friend of yours tells you that your client might suffer from a psychiatric condition known as "Munchausen's syndrome by proxy." You hope to use this information to consider presenting an insanity defense. (Courts)

    a.    Search the Internet for the term "Munchausen's syndrome by proxy." What is the definition?

    b.    Briefly explain whether or not your client's condition can fulfill the requirements of the various tests for the insanity defense.

- M'Naughten
- Irresistible Impulse
- Durham
- Substantial Capacity
- Federal Comprehensive Crime Control Act

24. Exercise: **The Fourth Amendment and the Exclusionary Rule**

A woman called the police to her home after her daughter was severely beaten earlier in the day by the daughter's boyfriend. The daughter agreed to use her key to let the officers into the apartment where the man was sleeping. The officers did not seek to obtain either an arrest warrant or a search warrant. After the daughter unlocked the apartment door, the officers entered and found a white substance, which later proved to be cocaine, sitting on a table. They arrested the sleeping man and charged him with narcotics offenses. The defendant sought to have the drugs excluded from evidence because the officers' warrantless search was based on permission from the girlfriend who had moved out of the apartment several weeks earlier and therefore had no authority to give the officers permission to enter and search. (Policing, Courts)

a. As the prosecutor, think about possible exceptions to the exclusionary rule, such as those discussed for the Fourth and Fifth Amendments, to make arguments about why the evidence should not be excluded.

b. Now, imagine that you are the judge. Decide whether the evidence obtained in the warrantless search should be excluded. Provide reasons for your decision. Consider the words of the Fourth Amendment, the purposes of the Amendment, and the potential effects on society from the rule you formulate for this case.

25. Exercise: **The Fifth and Sixth Amendments**

After arresting a suspect for burglary, police officers learned that the suspect's nickname was "Butch." A confidential informant had previously told them that someone named "Butch" was guilty of an unsolved murder in another city. The police in the other city were informed about this coincidence and they sent officers to question the suspect about the murder. Meanwhile, the suspect's sister secured the services of a lawyer to represent her brother on the burglary charge. Neither she nor the lawyer knew about the suspicions concerning the unsolved murder case. The lawyer telephoned the police station and said she would come to the station to be present if the police wished to question her client. The lawyer was told that the police would not question him until the following morning and she could come to the station at that time. Meanwhile, the police from the other city arrived and initiated the first of a series of evening questioning sessions with the suspect. The suspect was not informed that his sister had obtained the services of a lawyer to represent him. The suspect was not told that the lawyer had called the police and asked to be present during any questioning. During questioning, the suspect was informed of his Miranda rights, waived his right to be represented by counsel during questioning, and subsequently confessed to the murder. (Policing, Courts)

   a.   If you were the defense attorney, what arguments would you make to have the confession excluded from evidence?

   b.   If you were the judge, would you permit the confession to be used in evidence? Provide reasons for your decision.

26. Divide the class into small groups and have the students debate the constitutionality of **DNA "fingerprinting."** Does this violate the right to privacy? How could DNA information be used unethically? Ask the students if they favor DNA use by police. What are the advantages and disadvantages? (Policing, Criminal Investigation)

27. Have the students discuss the variety of **warrantless searches** that are legal under case law established by the U. S. Supreme Court. Should the Court expand warrantless searches into other areas in light of the "War on Terrorism?" (Policing, Terrorism and Homeland Security, Investigation, Criminal Investigation)

28. Divide the students into teams to prepare arguments about **constitutional issues affecting police practices**. Two teams can square off against each other to debate the proposition: The **exclusionary rule** is necessary to ensure that people's rights are protected against unreasonable searches and seizures. Another set of teams can debate each other about the proposition: **Miranda warnings** are not necessary because they are not actually required by the Constitution and they do little to protect criminal suspects. In the course of examining these issues, the students may be forced to see more clearly both sides of the continuing debates about these important criminal justice issues. (Policing, Criminal Investigation)

29. Exercise: **The Justification for Warrantless Searches**

Warrantless searches are important for police officers in regard to gathering evidence that might otherwise be lost or endanger the safety of others in society. In the following exercise, students should list the basis for justifying the warrantless searches listed below. (Policing, Criminal Investigation)

a. What purpose(s) are served by allowing law enforcement officers to conduct a search without a warrant?

b. Are these searches justified in violating a person's rights based upon the purposes that you listed?

- Stop and Frisk on the Streets
- Warrantless Search of Hispanics five miles from the Mexican border
- Search Incident to a Lawful Arrest
- Automobile Searches
- Searching through someone's luggage at the airport
- Consent searches

30. Debate whether a **DNA database** should be developed to solve crime more rapidly. What are the implications in terms of privacy and constitutional rights? (Criminal Investigation)

31. Ask the class to discuss the question **"Should juveniles receive the death penalty for murder"**? As the students explore the question, their attention should be directed to the philosophical underpinnings of juvenile justice which dictate that juvenile offenders should be treated differently than adults with respect to culpability and punishment.

In particular, competing goals of retribution, incapacitation, deterrence, and rehabilitation come into sharp focus when considering which objectives are arguably advanced by executing or not executing juvenile murderers. Should there be a cut-off age for juvenile's eligibility for the death penalty? If a nine year old intentionally takes his parents' gun and shoots another child because of a dispute over baseball cards, should that child be subject to the death penalty? Is there any specific age that is too young to be subject to the death penalty? Does it depend on the heinousness of the crime or upon the characteristics of an individual child? Finally, if children can be subject to the death penalty, then is there any reason to treat children differently than adults by having a separate juvenile justice system? (Juvenile Justice)

32. Have the students debate whether a person under eighteen years of age should be **tried as an adult**. What types of crime would require a juvenile to be tried in adult court? (Juvenile Justice)

33. Discuss, compare, and contrast **civil and criminal law proceedings**.

    Some main points: Who has been harmed, prosecution, penalties, and procedural differences (burden of proof). Civil law remedies private wrongs. The criminal law punishes wrongs against society.

34. List and discuss the **elements of a crime**.

    Some main points: The elements include the guilty act, guilty intent, that the actus reus and mens rea be related, and may also include attendant circumstances and/or specific results. For instance, an intentional (mens rea) murder results in death of a person.

35. Discuss and explain Amendments from the **Bill of Rights** pertinent to criminal procedure.

    Some main points: Fourth Amendment: protection from unreasonable searches and seizures, Fifth Amendment: protection against self-incrimination, Sixth Amendment: right to counsel and trial by jury, and Eighth Amendment: prohibition against cruel and unusual punishment. These rights are the basis for the protection of defendants' due process rights in criminal procedures.

36. List and discuss the **4 main sources of law**. Be sure to provide examples. Which source is supreme?

    Some main points: Constitutions, statutes, administrative regulations, and court decisions. Each of these may be state or federal. The U.S. Constitution is the supreme law of the land.

37. Briefly explain the recent trend in the **Supreme Court's treatment/ philosophy of cases regarding criminal rules of evidence**.

    Some main points: The current trend regarding criminal rules of evidence, as treated by the Court, has been one of minimizing or decreasing the breadth of both the exclusionary rule and *Miranda*.

Both the Burger and Rehnquist Courts have generally worked to carve out exceptions to the exclusionary rule and *Miranda*.

38. Briefly define the **exclusionary rule**. Discuss the three rationales justifying the exclusionary rule. Be sure to provide examples.

    Some main points: The exclusionary rule prohibits a prosecutor from using illegally obtained evidence in court. 1. A court should not participate in or condone illegal conduct. 2. Excluding evidence will deter illegal conduct by law enforcement. 3. Alternative methods to deter police misconduct have been unworkable.

39. In general, have **criminal rules of evidence** significantly reduced the power of the courts and police? What is the general consensus? What is your opinion? Be sure to explain your position.

    Some main points: In general, criminal rules of evidence, such as the exclusionary rule and *Miranda*, have not significantly hurt the criminal justice system. Most research has found that less than 5% of cases are rejected for search and seizure reasons. Defense attorneys file motions to suppress evidence in less than 8% of all cases and such motions are rarely granted (approximately 10% of the time). Thus, such rules are only a minor source of case attrition.

40. Consult your states rules or code of **criminal procedure on plea bargaining and the entry of guilty pleas**. Do these rules provide any enough protection for defendants and any for crime victims? (Victimization)

41. Exercise: **Court-made Law.**

    Should courts have the power to create crimes? What are the pros and cons of such powers? What is your opinion on the matter?

    Possible discussion points: Pro – provides flexibility to cover new crimes, prevents culpable people from escaping because legislature missed something, protects public. Con – due process fair notice, possible discriminatory or arbitrary action by judges, seems contrary to rule of law.

42. How seriously are we committed to the **principle of limited means**? Haven't we gotten to the point where we expect that every

problem will be solved quickly by passing a criminal law? Have we become too dependent on government to solve all problems?

Possible discussion points: It can be argued that the principle of limited means is an outmoded philosophical concept which does not reflect needs of people in a modern society. There are too many threats to public safety. Growth of the law and the state are inevitable in advanced industrial societies. Exponential growth of law and litigation indicates people are unable or unwilling to settle disputes informally. On the other hand, the informal agents of social control are being superseded and weakened as people become dependent on government. People see no need to maintain the social fabric as the government is increasingly called upon to maintain order. People who are dependent on government will be less likely to challenge abuses by government, and Constitutional rights will eventually fade away. The Patriot Act and treatment of Guantanamo detainees are the handwriting on wall.

43. Define and describe *mens rea*, *actus reus*, **and concurrence**. Provide an example of each.

Some main points: *Mens rea* is the intent or mental element of a crime. "Intentionally" is an example. The *actus reus* is the act element. Any kind of voluntary act or omission, such as failure to stop at the scene of an accident could be an act. Concurrence means that the act must flow from or be caused by the *mens rea*.

44. What two limits are imposed on government power to punish by the **Eighth Amendment**? Be sure to provide examples.

Some main points: The two limits are a ban on barbarous punishments such as torture and the requirement that punishments be proportional to the crime.

45. What are the three levels of scrutiny under **equal protection**, and to what types of classifications does each apply? Explain each test.

Some main points: Classifications based on race, ethnicity, national origin, and religion are subject to strict scrutiny. Gender classifications are subject to intermediate scrutiny. All other classifications are subject to minimal scrutiny or the rational basis test.

46. Exercise: **Vagueness of Law.**

What are the two concerns that are implicated by laws that are vague? Give an example of each concern. Why is some vagueness inevitable in any law?

Some main points: The two concerns are fair notice to citizens of what is criminal and the potential for discriminatory or arbitrary enforcement. Human language can never be perfectly clear or cover all possible contingencies. Laws that prohibit "loitering" are void for vagueness.

47. Explain the principle of **proportionality** and provide examples.

Some main points: The Eighth Amendment ban on cruel and unusual punishments requires that the punishment fit (be proportional to) the crime (the harm committed). Minor crimes cannot receive severe punishments. The death penalty for burglary would obviously be an example.

48. Why do we require a criminal act for **criminal liability**? Why not punish people for just thinking about committing crimes?

Possible discussion points: Everyone now and again has thoughts or fantasies about behavior that would be criminal. No society can afford to prosecute all its members. Unless the person admitted the bad thoughts, how would we prove they had such thoughts? Further, the requirement of an act limits the power of government.

49 Define, compare, and contrast **crimes of criminal conduct and crimes causing criminal harm**. Provide an example of each.

Some main points: A crime of criminal conduct has only three elements: *mens rea*, concurrence and *actus reus*. A crime of causing criminal harm has five elements: *mens rea*, concurrence, *actus reus*, causation and resulting harm. Murder is an example of a crime of criminal harm.

50. What are the three ways that a **legal duty** can be created such that omission to perform the duty can be a criminal act? Provide examples of each.

Some main points: The three sources of legal duties are statutes, contracts and special relationships.

51. Go to the Penal Code, Criminal Code or criminal statutes for your home state. Do these statutes use a fixed set of intent or **culpability terms** and definitions (as in the Model Penal Code), or are there a wide variety of terms used for the mens rea element?

   Possible discussion points: Some states use the Model Penal levels of culpability. Others, such Texas, use a similar but not identical scheme.

52. What are **intervening causes** and how do they affect a defendant's responsibility? Be sure to provide examples. (Courts)

   Some main points: If a crime has a harm or result element, the prosecution must prove that the defendant caused the harm beyond a reasonable doubt. The prosecution must prove that the defendant's acts were both (1) the cause in fact (but for cause) and (2) the proximate or legal cause. Cause in fact is an empirical or factual issue. Proximate or legal cause involves the question of whether it is fair or just to make the defendant responsible for a harm that occurred in an unusual fashion. For instance, sometimes a defendant will do an act and start a chain of events in motion, but some other event will occur after the defendant's act and contribute to causation of the harm. In general, if this intervening cause was normal and foreseeable, the defendant will not be relieved of liability for the harm.

53. What is *mens rea*? Why is it important for a crime to have a *mens rea* element? How does the *mens rea* element in a crime relate to other elements?

   Some main points: Most crimes have *a mens rea* or mental element that must be proven by the prosecution beyond a reasonable doubt. The basic idea is that it is not fair to punish someone unless they had some form of mental fault or blameworthiness. The mental element can apply to or modify other elements of a crime and thus a crime can have more than one mental element. For instance, the *mens rea* can apply to the act, the harm, or the circumstances.

54. When we make an individual **vicariously liable** for a strict liability offense, aren't we in fact sacrificing this individual for the sake of the greater good of the community? Does the difficulty of getting convictions for certain types of offenses justify this?

Possible discussion points: These statutes can be visualized as such and thus seem inconsistent with America's emphasis on the importance of the individual. On the other hand, without such laws, wouldn't the public be at risk?

55. Why does government find it necessary to **use vicarious liability and strict liability crimes** to fight corporate crime? Be sure to provide examples.

    Some major points: *Mens rea* in business crimes is hard to prove because of the size and complexity of organizations and decision-making. Legislatures attempt to overcome this by creating strict liability crimes (eliminating any *mens rea*) and/or creating vicarious liability. Vicarious liability raises due process constitutional issues and policy questions about its effectiveness.

56. What are the four elements of most **accessory-after-the-fact statutes**? Provide an example of each element.

    Some main points: First, the accessory personally aided the criminal. Second, the accessory knew a felony was committed. Third, the accessory aided the criminal for the purpose of hindering prosecution of the criminal. Fourth, the accessory did not commit the felony.

57. Discuss the mens rea and *actus reus* of **accomplice liability**. Discuss some of the differences that might be found between jurisdictions.

    Some main points: The essence of accomplice *actus reus* is that the accomplice took some positive action to aid or assist in the commission of a crime actually committed by another. The *mens rea* of complicity varies; depending on the jurisdiction. Some jurisdictions require only a general intent. Others require that the accomplice had some desire or intent to see the crime committed. Further, the *mens rea* may be purpose, knowledge, recklessness, or negligence.

58. Look in the Crimes Code or Penal Code for the state in which you reside and/or go to college. How does the **general attempt statute** define the *actus reus* of attempt? Do you think this is a good definition to use?

59. Define, describe, compare and contrast **attempt, solicitation and conspiracy**. Be sure to provide an example of each.

Some main points: A criminal attempt is a crime of starting but not completing some contemplated crime. A criminal conspiracy is the crime of agreeing to commit some planned crime. Criminal solicitation involves inducing, asking, or hiring someone to commit a crime.

60. What are the two rationales for the crime of **attempt**? Provide an example of each.

Some main points: Criminal liability for criminal attempt offenses is based on two rationales: First, is preventing dangerous conduct and second is neutralizing dangerous people. The *mens rea* of inchoate crimes is the specific intent to commit a complete crime.

61. What are the three basic kinds of **defenses**? Be sure to give an example of each.

Some main points: There are three kinds of defenses. The three are alibis, justifications, and excuses. Alibis free defendants from criminal liability, because they prove it's impossible for the defendants to have committed the crime because they were somewhere else at the time of the crime. Justifications free defendants from criminal liability, because they prove the defendants aren't blameworthy. Doing the criminal act was right or justified. An example is self-defense. Excuses free defendants from criminal liability, because they prove the defendants aren't responsible for their acts. An example is the insanity defense.

62. Discuss the general rules on the **use of force and deadly force**. Be sure to provide examples.

Some main points: According to the rule of law, the government has a monopoly on the use of force. Individuals may use force only when authorized by law. Self-defense is a concession to necessity and is only justified when the force is reasonably and immediately necessary for defense. Deadly force is justified only when the necessity is unprovoked and the attack involves threatened death or serious bodily injury. The amount of force used must be the minimum amount reasonably necessary to defend against an imminent threat.

63. Discuss, define, compare and contrast the four major **tests of insanity**. Which one do you think is the best? Be sure to explain your position.

Some main points: There are four main tests of the insanity defense. The right-wrong (M'Naghten) test focuses on defects in reason. The product-of-mental illness test (Durham rule) focuses on criminal acts resulting from (are the product of) mental disease. The irresistible impulse test focuses on defects in volition or self-control. The substantial capacity test (Model Penal Code) focuses on reason and self-control. Insanity is an affirmative defense in which the actual burden of proof varies, depending on the jurisdiction.

64. What impact did the acquittal of John Hinckley have on the **insanity defense** in the U.S.? Be sure to provide examples.

John Hinckley, who attempted to assassinate President Reagan was found not guilty by reason of insanity. This verdict troubled many and may have been caused by the fact that the prosecution was required to prove that Hinckley was sane beyond a reasonable doubt. Subsequent federal legislation places the burden on the defendant to prove their insanity by clear and convincing evidence. Some states also changed their law to place the burden of proof on the defendant. The federal government shifted the burden of proof to the defendant by clear and convincing evidence and eliminated any volitional test of insanity.

65. Does the jurisdiction in which you reside or attend college have the **death penalty**? If, so what are the aggravating or mitigating factors that determine whether the death penalty will be imposed? (Punishment and Sentencing)

Possible Discussion Points: Over half the states have a death penalty. Typical aggravating factors are murdering a person the offender knows is a peace officer, and committing the murder during the course of a rape or kidnapping.

66. How many types of **murder** are there in the law of the jurisdiction in which you reside or attend college?

Possible Discussion Points: Most states have four basic types of murder: first degree murder, second degree murder, voluntary

137

manslaughter and involuntary manslaughter. Grading murder into first and second degree is important because in some states only first-degree (or capital) murders qualify for the death penalty (or prison for life without parole in states without the death penalty). Second degree murder is typically an unpremeditated but intentional killing. Many jurisdictions, including Texas have criminal homicide statutes covering killings while the defendant was driving a vehicle or operating a boat while intoxicated.

67. Define, discuss, compare and contrast **voluntary and involuntary manslaughter.**

Some main points: A voluntary manslaughter is an intentional, sudden killing triggered by an adequate provocation. Provocation isn't an excuse for criminal homicide; it only reduces the punishment to allow for human weaknesses. Most jurisdictions have both objective and subjective requirements for the elements of voluntary manslaughter. Only certain types of provocation are deemed legally adequate. Usually these are mutual combat, assault and battery, trespass and adultery. Words alone are almost never deemed an adequate provocation. Catching a spouse in the act of adultery is generally recognized as an adequate provocation. Further, the killer must not have cooled off from the sudden passion. If the killer did cool off, it is an intentional murder and not a voluntary manslaughter. Specifically, the elements of voluntary manslaughter are as follows. The *actus reus* is killing of another person. The *mens rea* is intent to kill or inflict serious bodily injury. The circumstances are sudden heat of passion flowing from an adequate provocation (or honest but unreasonable belief that killing was necessary in self-defense). The acts must cause the death of another.

Involuntary manslaughter is the least blameworthy form of criminal homicide. It involves unintentional (reckless or negligent) killing. Recklessness involves conscious creation of a serous and unjustifiable risk. Negligence involves unknowing creation of a substantial and unjustifiable risk.

68. Most states today have four main types of **criminal homicide.** Define and discuss these and provide examples.

Some main points: Most states have four basic types of murder: first degree murder, second degree murder, voluntary manslaughter and involuntary manslaughter. Grading murder into first and second degree is important because in some states only first-degree (or capital) murders qualify for the death penalty (or prison for life without parole in states without the death penalty). Second degree murder is typically an unpremeditated but intentional killing.

69. Consult the **statutory rape or sexual assault statute** in the state where you live or go to college. What is the age of consent (the age at which the person can no longer be the victim of a statutory rape)? Do you think that age is too high or too low?

    Some discussion points: The age of consent in Texas is seventeen. The ages in most states are in the range of fifteen to seventeen. It can be argued that such laws interfere with the right of young people to choose their sex partners. Further, if there are no STD or pregnancy problems, why should the state be intervening?

70. How has the law of **rape and rape prosecutions** changed over the years?

    Much of the law of rape and rape prosecutions has changed over the years. The marital exception and prompt report rule have been abolished in many jurisdictions. Corroboration of the victim's testimony is no longer required. Rape shield laws limit the ability of the defense to bring out evidence of the victim's prior sex life. Utmost resistance by the victim is no longer required. Reasonable resistance is enough.

71. The law of theft and burglary are good examples of law that has evolved as society changes. What other **changes in the criminal law**, or law in general, can you think of that also reflect changes in society?

    Possible discussion points: The law regarding rape has changed as females have gained more power in society. The First Amendment has had to evolve to deal with cyberspace.

72. After computers and the Internet, what will be the next major change in society that will necessitate **major changes or additions to our criminal law**?

Possible discussion points: Many argue that the technology of surveillance has expanded rapidly endangering our right to privacy from both private and governmental intrusion. New laws may be needed to protect us. Other possible changes are demographic (elderly and children of the poor).

73. What types of criminal and civil laws have been used to try to deal with **gang problems**? (Gangs)

Some main points: A number of state and city governments have passed criminal laws to regulate gang behavior. In some places, it's a crime to participate in a gang. Some statutes and ordinances have stiffened the penalties for crimes committed by gang members. Others make it a crime to encourage minors to participate in gangs. Some have applied organized crime statutes to gangs. A few have punished parents for their children's gang activities. Cities have also passed ordinances banning gang members from certain public places, particularly city parks.

In addition to criminal penalties, cities have also turned to civil remedies to control gang activity. For example, in the ancient civil remedy injunction to abate public nuisances, which is still used, government attorneys ask courts to declare gang activities and gang members public nuisances and to issue injunctions (court orders) to abate (stop) the public nuisance.

74. Describe two terrorist events since 1994 that have had a major impact on **anti-terrorism laws**. Name one congressional act in response to each. Briefly discuss some of the provisions of these laws. (Terrorism and Homeland Security)

Some main points: The bombing of the Federal Building in 1995 prompted Congress to pass the Anti-Terrorism and Effective Death Penalty Act (AEDPA). The terrorist attacks involving airliners on Sept. 11, 2001 prompted passage of the U.S.A. Patriot Act.

75. What are some of the acts that are criminalized by recent **anti-terrorist legislation**? What are some of the constitutional objections to some of this legislation? (Terrorism and Homeland Security)

Some main points: It is a federal crime to harbor or conceal terrorists. It is also a crime to provide material support to terrorists and terrorist organizations. These laws are frequently challenged on the basis of void-for-vagueness and interfering with First Amendment rights of association.

76. A variety of **mental disorders** have been linked to criminal activities. Have students discuss whether those criminals who have been deemed mentally ill should be incarcerated for their offenses or be housed in a mental health facility. Is it appropriate to incarcerate someone with a mental illness? Are they "getting away" with the crime if they are housed in a mental health facility instead of a prison? (Criminology)

77. **Searching of Automobiles:** Students always express interest in the ability of police officers to stop and search their automobiles. Have students discuss the circumstances under which this occurred to them and then discuss the legal issues that made this an appropriate response for the officer. (Policing)

78. **Crime Trends:** Have each student select one type of crime. They should provide the legal definition for the offense, incidence rates at both the state and national levels, and clearance rates at both the state and national levels. To what extent does this crime in your state reflect nationwide trends? (Criminology)

79. **Insanity and the Law:** Have your students look up the case of John Hinckley shooting President Ronald Reagan. Explore his motives and rationalizations and try to determine if this was the act of a sane man or an assassin. (Criminology)

### Punishment and Sentencing

1. Seek permission from the local criminal court to **follow a case** through the formal criminal justice system. Develop a paper based on this case study. (Criminal Justice)

2. Invite a judge to come to class to discuss the differences between **criminal law and civil law**. (Criminal Law)

3. Prior to discussing the **insanity defense**, have students discuss their perception of it. Encourage a discussion of whether they think it is easy to claim the insanity defense. (Criminal Law)

4. Invite a judge to class to discuss the different types of **criminal defenses** discussed in the text. (Criminal Law)

5. Develop a research paper on the use of **the insanity defense**, using particular cases to illustrate the use of the different tests of insanity. (Criminal Law)

6. Develop a research paper on the various **excuse defenses** discussed in the text. (Criminal Law)

7. **Preventive detention** has been a source of concern for civil libertarians who believe that it violates the due process clause of the U.S. Constitution, since it means that a person will be held in custody before proven guilty. Encourage student discussion of this issue.

8. What does your state or federal legislator think should be the **purpose of punishment**? After all, that person makes the laws. Look in the newspaper files at election time to see where he or she stood on these issues. If there was no issue here, why? (Courts)

9. Divide the class into small groups. The groups will act as sentencing judges in **determining appropriate punishments** for several hypothetical criminal offenders. The judges have complete discretion to pronounce sentences ranging from fines and probation to terms of incarceration to the death penalty. As the judges within each group seek to reach a consensus about the appropriate punishment in each case, they should consciously seek to identify the factors and considerations that lead them to their conclusions (e.g., characteristics of offender, characteristics of the crime, purpose of criminal sanction, etc.).

   After each group has reached a consensus for each case, the entire class should compare the different outcomes produced by each group. The class should also compare each group's results with the results produced by the Minnesota sentencing guidelines. What accounts for the differences between student groups and the differences between the students and the policy makers in Minnesota?

   Case #1: A woman shot and killed her husband as he took a nap on the living room sofa. She claimed that her husband was physically abusive and that she lived in fear for her life. She presented witnesses who testified that her husband periodically threatened her and struck her during fits of anger. The jury convicted her of second degree murder (homicide with intent but not the requisite degree of premeditation). The prosecutor recommends that she serve at least ten years.

Case #2: A nineteen year old man was arrested inside a home at night after the people next door heard suspicious noises in the house of their vacationing neighbors. The man entered by breaking a window and he was caught putting jewelry and small appliances into pillow cases. He had two prior convictions on his record, one for shoplifting which resulted in probation and one for simple robbery (purse snatching) that resulted in serving 30 days in county jail. The man entered a quick guilty plea to burglary charges and begged the judge to send him to a drug rehabilitation program to help him gain control over his cocaine habit. The prosecutor recommends that he serve at least seven years.

Cases #3: A college student pleaded guilty to selling marijuana after he sold a small bag of dope (sandwich bag size) to an undercover police officer outside of a bar on a Saturday night. The student has no prior criminal record, is the son of a Presbyterian minister, and is an honors student in philosophy at the local college. The prosecutor recommends that he serve at least sixty days in county jail.

Case #4: A woman pleaded guilty to the unauthorized use of a motor vehicle. She lived with her three children in a rundown downtown apartment building. She and her children were supported by food stamps and other forms of government assistance. When her three-year-old daughter seemed to have a fever one night, the woman went downstairs to the busy intersection and hailed a taxi cab. The cabdriver refused to take her and the child to the hospital because she had no money. While arguing with the cabdriver on the sidewalk, she pushed the driver, grabbed his car keys, and drove her daughter to the hospital herself in the taxi. The hospital personnel could find nothing wrong with the child. In exchange for dropping assault charges, the woman entered a guilty plea to the unauthorized use of an automobile charge. She has two prior convictions for misdemeanor shoplifting.

The prosecutor recommends that she serve at least six months in county jail.

10. Have the students debate the constitutionality of the **death penalty** for the following defendants who each have committed heinous murders. This should illustrate to the students the difficult question of drawing a line between life and death:

Which of these defendants should receive the death penalty?

Case #1: mildly retarded person

Case #2: moderately retarded person

Case #3: severely retarded person

Case #4: seventeen year old male

Case #5: seventeen year old female

Case #6: fifteen year old male

Case #7: fifteen year old female

Case #8: accomplice to a murder who did not actually commit the murder (i.e. driving the getaway car or kidnapping a person who was ultimately murdered)

11. Exercise: **Forms of the Criminal Sanction**

Discuss whether and how the underlying purposes of the criminal sanction fit with various forms of punishment. Ask yourself: Does this form of punishment effectively advance any or all of the underlying purposes?

For each punishment, comment on the pros and cons of all of the following: rehabilitation, deterrence, incapacitation, and retribution.

a. Incarceration
b. Probation
c. Fines
d. Capital Punishment
e. Community Service

12. Exercise: **Sentencing**

Imagine that you are a judge deciding on sentences for individuals who have entered guilty pleas in the following situations. What sentence would you impose?

a. A nineteen-year-old high school dropout pleads guilty to burglary. He broke into a home and was caught carrying a VCR out the window when the homeowners awoke from the noise of someone in their living room. He has one previous felony conviction for burglary.

b. A college senior who was caught copying copyrighted computer software from a university computer system onto his own diskette without permission. The value of the software was $700. The student entered a guilty plea to a simple theft charge with an agreement that the prosecutor would recommend leniency. The student has been suspended from college for one year by the school's disciplinary board.

c. A man who recently completed a prison sentence for armed robbery killed a man during an argument at a bar. The defendant claimed that the victim owed him money so he went to the bar with a knife in order to scare the victim. A confrontation between the two developed into a fight and the victim was stabbed to death. The defendant entered a guilty plea to the charge of second-degree murder. He has served prior prison terms for two armed robbery convictions.

Now look at the sentencing guidelines in your area. What would be the sentence for each offender under the guidelines? Do you think the guidelines are too harsh, too lenient, or just right? Explain.

13. Have students write an essay on what they believe to be the **most important goal of punishment**. Select a few of the excellent essays and read to the class the types of arguments developed by the students. Finally, have the students discuss which arguments they found to be the most compelling and why. (Corrections)

14. If possible, invite a state legislator or local prosecutor who is involved in corrections to discuss with the class the **role of politics in determining sentencing policy**. Have the legislator discuss the

positive and negative aspects that politics have on the sentencing process of the state.

15. Divide the class into three groups – those who support the **death penalty**, those who do not, and a neutral judging group. Have the pro and con groups select a representative who will argue for them on the relevant issues in front of the judging group. After the issues have been presented, the judging group selects the group with the most persuasive arguments and explains why.

16. Have students design and administer a short questionnaire regarding opinions on the use of **intermediate sanctions**. The questions can be a "favor-oppose" format pairing specific sanctions with specific crimes. Have the class discuss the results and implications of their findings. (Community Corrections and Probation)

17. Develop case histories for several offenders for various criminal acts. Make certain there are at least four offenders in each crime category, each with differing family histories, criminal records and connections to the community. Divide the class into teams of "probation officers" for the purpose of writing up brief **PSIs** for each offender. Make this a group out of class assignment. Then, have a class debate, requiring each team to defend their position. If you wish, appoint three members of the class as judges who must read each report and will then render a group verdict on each offender. (Corrections)

18. Take your class on a field trip to a local municipal, district or similar typically misdemeanor court (for arraignment and sentencing) and which also has felony jurisdiction for first appearance and/or preliminary hearing. After watching at least two hours of **release and sentencing decisions**, hold a discussion in class to debate the justifications for decisions witnessed. Invite the judge to comment to the class about the factors in making such decisions. (Courts)

19. Invite a local judge to class to discuss the importance of the **pre-sentence investigation report** on sentencing. Have the judge comment on what weight is given to the report among his/her fellow judges. In addition, have the judge discuss the future role of

pre-sentence investigation reports in the local judiciary. (Community Corrections and Probation)

20. Have the students go to their state's department of correction website. Have them gather information as to the race of the inmates currently incarcerated. Have them discuss their views on why there are so many **minorities incarcerated**. (Race, Incarceration and Prison Society)

21. Have the class develop and administer a public-opinion questionnaire on the use of **capital punishment**. Include questions from other surveys. Compare results.

22. Invite a prison administrator from a prison with a death row to discuss his/her views on **capital punishment**. Review your state's policies for carrying out an execution. (Incarceration and Prison Society)

23. Should **victims** play a larger role in the criminal justice system? To what extent should victims play a role in the prosecution and punishment of their assailants? (Victimization)

    Possible discussion points: Victim impact statements, victim's wishes in sentencing, mandatory victim testimony, victims advocates as part of the courtroom work group.

24. Interview a criminal court judge or ask such a judge to make a presentation to the class about **sentencing, prison overcrowding**, etc. (Courts)

    Possible discussion points: Many judges will say that sentencing is one of the toughest parts of the job. Some may welcome the limitation of their discretion. However, most judges will probably be unhappy if their discretion is severely limited. Federal judges have been complaining about the sentencing guidelines for years.

25. Define, discuss, compare and contrast **determinate and indeterminate sentences**. Be sure to provide examples.

    Some main points: Determinate sentence – specific number of years imprisonment imposed. Indeterminate sentence – judge imposes sentence range, parole board decides when inmate will be released.

26. Define, discuss, compare and contrast **sentencing disparity and sentencing discrimination**.

   Some main points: Discriminatory sentencing is sentencing which is based on illegal considerations such as race, ethnicity, gender etc. Numerous studies have probed the extent to which economic status, age, gender, and race improperly influence the sentence. The results of such studies are mixed. Disparity refers to inconsistencies in sentencing. There is disparity between states because of state law, and judicial backgrounds and attitudes contribute to disparity.

27. What are some of the criticisms of increased **sentencing severity**? Do you agree or disagree with these criticisms? Explain your position.

   Some main points: Prison populations are increasing, and prison only makes most offenders worse—not better. The United States sends more people to prison than any other Western nation, and the rate of incarceration is increasing steadily. The result is severe prison overcrowding, compounded by federal court orders requiring major improvements in prison conditions. The financial costs of such mass imprisonment are staggering. Although taxpayers want longer and harsher sentences, they are unwilling to spend the large sums of money needed to build adequate facilities and provide programs for inmates.

28. Explain and discuss **sentencing guidelines**. What is their purpose, and what has been their impact?

   Some main points: Sentencing guidelines attempt to control judicial discretion and answer charges that sentences are too lenient. There are two types of guidelines. Voluntary or recommended guidelines are not mandatory. Presumptive or mandatory guidelines must be followed by judges. Voluntary guidelines have had little impact, but mandatory guidelines have changed judicial behavior and have resulted in more severe sentences.

   However, the Eighth Amendment prohibits execution of the mentally retarded and those under fifteen years of age when the crime was committed. It also appears that murder may be the only crime for which this penalty can be exacted.

29. Does the jurisdiction in which you reside or attend college have the **death penalty**? If, so what are the aggravating or mitigating factors that determine whether the death penalty will be imposed? (Criminal Law)

    Possible Discussion Points: Over half the states have a death penalty. Typical aggravating factors are murdering a person the offender knows is a peace officer, and committing the murder during the course of a rape or kidnapping.

30. Exercise: **Court case strength**

    Break the class into groups and have them discuss the following questions:

    a.  What would make a strong case, as opposed to a weak case, against a suspect for burglary, based on both facts and case file?

    b.  Why is non-verbal communication important when testifying to a jury, and what other suggestions can they come up with for a testifying officer make a positive impression on the jury, other than those made in the text?

31. Break the class into groups. After a set preparation time, give each group five minutes to perform a **mock investigator presentation** with prosecution testimony and a defense cross-examination in front of the class.

32. Although most Americans support the **death penalty**, there remains an ongoing debate as to its effectiveness as a deterrent against murder. Divide the class into two groups. Have one group develop a presentation in support of the deterrent effect of capital punishment and the other group against the deterrent effect. Students, then, can discuss which position is the stronger of the two. (Criminology)

33. Divide the students into two groups. Have one develop an argument in support of the **death penalty** and have the other develop an argument against the death penalty. Discuss which side

is able to make the stronger case. How does one's own position on this topic impact his or her evaluation of the debate? (Courts)

34. Invite a local member of the ACLU to address the class regarding the **capital sentencing process** and ongoing reform/abolition efforts. (Race)

35. Moderate a class debate on **capital punishment**. (Race)

# CHAPTER 6

# CORRECTIONS

### Corrections

1. It has been said that "corrections is the tail that wags the dog of the justice system." This observation, of course, results from arrests, convictions, and sentencing being based on the amount of **resources in institutions and community corrections**. Do you think this is a valid observation? Please justify your opinion in a 1,500 word essay. Cite the sources for all data used.

2. It has been stated that **rehabilitation** is almost impossible in the abnormal world of the prison. In your opinion is it possible or not to develop normal, positively productive citizens in the prisons of today? Please give your opinion and provide two constructive suggestions which might help this situation in a 1,500 word essay and cite the sources for all data used. (Incarceration and Prison Society)

3. Right now, it is not generally necessary to have **highly educated (formal education) correctional officers**. Administrators often claim that all that is needed is training. What is your opinion about this issue? Are you in favor of increased education or not? Please include in your response the difference between education and training. Please give your opinion in a 1,500 word essay using data and cite the sources for all data used. (Careers)

4. Divide the class into small groups. The students are consultants for a state department of corrections. The state needs to build a new prison because of **overcrowding** at its aging correctional institutions.

The consultants' task is to design a new prison, including the physical layout of the building(s), plans for living space for the prisoners, and plans for programs and facilities. In designing the prison, the students need to consider a number of objectives:

a.  Making the facility safe and secure without employing an excessive number of staff personnel or otherwise producing excessive costs.

b.  Creating living conditions that meet constitutional standards for avoiding overcrowding and that create an environment that can be stable and controlled.

c.  Planning programs and facilities to achieve correctional goals. Because the state officials show great deference to the expert consultants, the consultants should also discuss and specify which goals (e.g., rehabilitation, incapacitation, retribution, etc.) their programs and facilities are intended to achieve.

After each group is finished, the entire class can compare the plans produced by each group. The exercise is intended to make students think seriously about the challenges that face corrections officials who must attempt to strike the appropriate balance between a variety of objectives: safety, security, staff morale, constitutional standards, rehabilitation, punishment, etc. (Incarceration and Prison Society)

5.  Debate the following question:

Has the correctional system within the United States become a **prison commercial complex**? Have a small group of students research this question from the perspective of corporations using government officials in order to profit from the "tough on crime" policies and have a separate group of students research the issue from the perspective of the prison system getting larger simply because the space is needed and must be developed due to the increased rate of incarceration. (Community Corrections and Probation, Incarceration and Prison Society)

6.  **Probation:** If you were a judge, what kinds of offenders would you put on probation?

What kinds of offenders would you not place on probation?

If you were a probation officer, which aspect of your job would receive your strongest emphasis: surveillance/rule enforcement or social services/counseling to help reintegration? Why?

If you were a judge, what conditions/restrictions would you impose on probationers? Why?

7. **Intermediate Sanctions:** Take the following intermediate sanctions and list them in order of the sanctions that you believe are most effective (1 for most effective and 8 for least effective). (Community Corrections and Probation)

   For each one, describe its strengths and weaknesses with respect to the goals that should be accomplished:

   a. Fines
   b. Restitution
   c. Boot camps
   d. Intensive probation supervision
   e. Forfeiture
   f. Day reporting centers
   g. Community service
   h. Home confinement

8. Discuss the **legacy of prisons**. What were prisons like in the 1940s and 1950s? 1960s and early 1970s? What has occurred in the last thirty years in the prison environment? (Incarceration and Prison Society)

9. Discuss the **goals of incarceration**. Which is most important? Why? (Incarceration and Prison Society)

10. For this exercise, students can be divided into small groups or the problem can be discussed as an entire class. Tell the students to imagine that they are members of an advisory committee that must quickly advise a new warden on steps to take to prevent a **gang war.**

    The warden is responsible for a new maximum security prison that is about to open. It is known that inmates being transferred to the prison include members of various gangs that have clashed in other institutions. There is a Mexican-American gang, an African-American gang, and a white gang. The new prison will also receive many of the state's youngest prisoners (ages 17-21) who were convicted for acts of violence. What steps should the warden take to minimize the prospects for violence? (Incarceration and Prison Society)

11. **Prisons and their Purposes:** If you were in charge of a state corrections department, how would you design your prisons? For each question, assume that the prisons have one primary purpose (listed below) and describe the physical design, policies, and programs that you would implement to help the institution advance the overriding goal. ? (Incarceration and Prison Society)

    a. Custodial Model
    b. Rehabilitation Model
    c. Reintegration Model

12. Exercise: **Prisoners' Rights: You are the Judge**

    Corrections officers at the main gate receive a report that a fight involving twelve prisoners has broken out in Cellblock C and that the corrections officers in Cellblock C are unable to break up the fight. Seven corrections officers run down the corridor from the main gate toward Cellblock C. As they round a corner, they practically run into inmate Joe Cottrell who is mopping and waxing the corridor floor. One officer grabs Cottrell by the shoulders and throws him aside while saying, "Get out of the way!" Cottrell falls into a wall, dislocates his shoulder, and later files a lawsuit against the officer by claiming that the rough treatment and resulting injury violated his Eighth Amendment right against cruel and unusual punishment. Were his Eighth Amendment rights violated? Explain.

    A prison chapel is used every Sunday for Christian services. A small group of prisoners reserve the chapel for each Tuesday evening where they meet to study an ancient religion from Asia that they claim to follow. For two years, they use the chapel every Tuesday to meditate and discuss books about their religion, and they do not cause any trouble. Then, one year, Christmas falls on a Wednesday, and the Asian religion group is told that they cannot have their meeting because the chapel is needed for a Christian Christmas eve service. They file a lawsuit claiming that their First Amendment right to free exercise of religion is being violated because they cannot use the chapel on Christmas Eve. Are their rights being violated? Explain. (Incarceration and Prison Society)

13. Debate the problem of **prisoners with HIV/AIDS**. Should prisoners be tested regularly and isolated because they might infect other prisoners? (Incarceration and Prison Society)

14. Take the students on a field trip to a **men's prison and a woman's prison**. Students should reflect on these experiences by comparing and contrasting the two types of prisons. (Incarceration and Prison Society)

15. Have the students debate whether ex-felons should be given the **right to vote**. (Community Corrections and Probation, Incarceration and Prison Society)

16. Over the course of the semester, collect articles in the local newspaper on issues pertaining to corrections. Identify and discuss how the issues affected individual correctional organizations and describe their effect on **the correctional system in your community or state**.

17. Have the student go to **various state Department of Corrections** websites. Have them write an essay on the size, security levels, breakdown of the population, and services provided by the correctional facilities. Have them compare the various states in class to spark a discussion regarding the differences between the states.

18. Supply students with a budget and have them **allocate funds for the three "Ps" of corrections** (probation, prison, and parole) at the local, state, county, or federal levels. Have students allocate the money and then have them identify what correctional goal (rehabilitation, retribution, incapacitation, and justice) was being stressed through their allocation of budgetary funds. What would be the possible effects on the community as a result of allocating funds in the manner that they did?

19. Have students contact departments of corrections to obtain **official policy, mission, and goal statements**. Compare and contrast these with the ideas of **early correctional reformers**.

20. In small groups, have students evaluate **the current state of corrections**. Discussions should include the most challenging problems facing corrections, the impact of historical developments, and the areas in need of new reforms.

21. Have students obtain and analyze information from the **American Corrections Association** regarding the organization's history, its principles and mission, and recent correctional reform efforts.

22. As a class project, have students design and administer a short questionnaire on **relevant and timely correctional issues**. Compare the responses of students in other courses and majors with those of the class.

23. Have students write an essay on what they believe to be **the most important goal of punishment.** Select a few of the excellent essays and read to the class the types of arguments developed by the students. Finally, have the students discuss which arguments they found to be the most compelling and why. (Punishment and Sentencing)

24. Develop case histories for several offenders for various criminal acts. Make certain there are at least four offenders in each crime category, each with differing family histories, criminal records and connections to the community. Divide the class into teams of "probation officers" for the purpose of writing up brief **PSIs** for each offender. Make this a group out of class assignment. Then, have a class debate, requiring each team to defend their position. If you wish, appoint three members of the class as judges who must read each report and will then render a group verdict on each offender. (Punishment and Sentencing)

25. If possible, invite an appellate court judge to explain the role the judiciary has had on the operations of correctional systems. Have the students write an essay on what they believe to be the proper **role of the judiciary in corrections**.

26. Have the local sheriff or warden attend class and discuss **jail overcrowding,** its consequences, and the types of offenders who make up the jail population. Have him/her comment on how state prison overcrowding and decriminalization of the mentally ill may have influenced the operations of the jail.

27. Visit the local jail and discuss with **the jail administrator** some of the problems in operating the facility. Discuss with the students in class possible solutions to these problems and the prospects of implementing them.

28. Contact a representative from a local philanthropic group that works in the jail. Ask this person to discuss with the class the **problems of implementing services in the jail** and possible solutions to these problems.

29. Contact a local vendor of correctional services to discuss the advantages and disadvantages of **privatization**. Have the students write an essay on what they thought were the most compelling arguments in the presentation. Read some essays in class to promote discussion of the issues. (Incarceration and Prison Society)

30. Construct a debate format among students with opposing sides on the following issues. (Incarceration and Prison Society)

   a. **Prison Compliance Mechanisms** – Coercive vs. Normative — (How should we encourage compliance?)

   b. **Prison Correctional Officer Positions** – Men vs. Women — (Who should govern inmates?)

31. Instruct students to go to the library and collect empirical literature on the **attitudes of correctional officers**. Have the students summarize and discuss implications of their findings in a policy-oriented paper assignment.

32. Contact the division of corrections in your state and obtain a list of **programs available within the prisons**. Have students debate which programs are the most beneficial to both the prisoner and society. (Incarceration and Prison Society)

33. Have a juvenile probation officer, prosecutor, and/or guardian ad litem/defense attorney come and speak to the class about the special problems in dealing with **juveniles in the criminal justice system**. (Juvenile Justice)

34. Have students discuss the issue of **overcrowding and the Eighth Amendment**. Is overcrowding a cruel and unusual punishment? What should be included in the minimum standards for confinement?

35. Break the class up into groups. Assign to each group a **correctional sanction**. Have each group present to the class the

positive and negative aspects of their correctional sanction. Then, cast votes as to which the group feels is most effective.

36. There are hundreds of **treatment and rehabilitation programs for offenders** that have been utilized in the past or are currently in favor. Have students identify one such program and provide an analysis of it. Specific topics to be discussed include the type of offender the program targets, the history of the program, its breadth of use across various facilities, its level of success, the length of the program, the structure of the program, etc.

37. Take the class on a tour of the **juvenile detention facility** in your locality. (Juvenile Justice)

## Community Corrections and Probation

1. Invite a **probation officer** to come to class and discuss his or her job duties. (Careers)

2. Arrange for students to do "ride-alongs" with **probation officers**.

3. Invite a judge to class to discuss issues involved in **granting and revoking probation**.

4. Obtain a copy of the **"typical" probation conditions** in your jurisdiction to share with the class. Encourage discussion of whether or not these conditions seem reasonable.

5. If possible, arrange for a **probationer** to come to class and discuss the terms of his or her probation.

6. Encourage student discussion of **electronic monitoring**. Do they view this sanction as a violation of First Amendment rights?

7. Encourage student discussion of **sentencing circles**. Are they supportive of this type of **restorative justice**? (Courts)

8. Develop a paper on the **legal issues surrounding probation**.

9. Develop a paper on the principles of **restorative justice**. (Courts)

10. Interview someone on probation and the **conditions of their probation**; develop a case study.

11. Develop a research paper on the pros and cons of **alternative correctional ideas.**

12. Invite a **juvenile probation officer** to come to class and discuss his or her job duties. Also have the probation officer discuss internship opportunities available for your students. (Juvenile Justice, Careers)

13. Look up the **standard conditions of probation in your jurisdiction.** What special conditions can also be added?

14. Interview a probationer to learn the **atmosphere of probation in your jurisdiction,** with appropriate permissions from the probation department or the court. (Try for a confidential interview.)

15. Obtain a **judge's view of probation and other alternatives** as described in the text.

16. It has been claimed that we are endangering the community by placing so many offenders in the community **without adequate probation supervision.** What do you think is the case? Comparing your local situation to the national situation, please address this issue and respond "yes" or "no." Please justify your opinion in a 1,500 word essay using data and cite the sources for all data used.

17. Debate the following question:

    Has the correctional system within the United States become a **prison commercial complex?** Have a small group of students research this question from the perspective of corporations using government officials in order to profit from the "tough on crime" policies and have a separate group of students research the issue from the perspective of the prison system getting larger simply because the space is needed and must be developed due to the increased rate of incarceration. (Corrections, Incarceration and Prison Society)

18. Have the students debate the **strengths and weaknesses of the probation system** in the U. S.

19. Let the entire class imagine that they are citizen-members of a **parole board.** Select five members of the class to be the "questioning members" who are permitted to ask questions to a

potential parolee. Have other class members play the roles of prisoners who are appearing before the parole board in order to seek release. When each prisoner appears before the class, strictly limit the questions to four minutes for each parole applicant.

After the four minutes of questioning, the entire class can vote on whether or not the person should be released on parole. After making several decisions, the class can discuss the thinking that guided their votes on each prisoner. Students should also discuss the questions that they would ask to parole applicants and the qualities that would lead them to grant parole.

The "prisoners" should memorize their profiles in order to answer questions "in character."

Parole applicant #1: An admitted heroin addict, age 33, who has served seven years of a ten-year sentence for armed robbery. He used a gun in the robbery of a convenience store. Prior to this prison sentence, he had been on probation for a series of theft offenses. The prisoner participated in substance abuse counseling and, except for two incidents five years ago of being caught attempting to make "home brew" from alcohol-based cough syrup and fruit juice, has never caused any disciplinary problems. He earned his GED in prison. He has been promised a job as a nighttime stock clerk at a discount department store near his old neighborhood. He has no family except a brother who also works at the discount department store.

Parole applicant #2: A college-educated, former bank manager, age 42, who was convicted of molesting boys in a Boy Scout troop for which he was the Scoutmaster. He has served three years of an eight-year sentence. He has been a "model prisoner," serving as a tutor for other prisoners in the GED program and organizing religious programs through the prison chapel. He was told upon sentencing that he must participate in a special sex abuse counseling program, but he is still on the waiting list to be transferred to the overcrowded special correctional facility that has such a program. He has voluntarily worked with the counselor in prison, but this counselor has no special training in sex abuse treatment programs. He has been promised a job as a bookkeeper

160

in an insurance company managed by his old college roommate. His wife divorced him and took their children.

Parole applicant #3: A twenty-two year old high school dropout who has served three years of an eight-year sentence for shooting and seriously injuring a member of a rival gang. He had a long record of arrests and convictions for lesser offenses of assault, vandalism, weapons possession, and possession of stolen property. He was suspected of being involved in gang-related drug trafficking prior to imprisonment. Although he did not commit any major disciplinary infractions in prison, he spent his time with members of his old gang, many of whom frequently caused trouble inside the prison. He is suspected of participating in a gang-related assault in the prison, but no prisoners who witnessed the event have been willing to provide information. He has not participated in any prison programs, except for spending many hours lifting weights in the recreation program. He has been promised a job unloading trucks at a warehouse.

Parole applicant #4: A woman with many previous convictions for prostitution and drug possession who was convicted of killing a man believed to be one of her customers. She stabbed him and then shot him after he was seriously injured by the knife wound. She claimed that she acted in self-defense but a jury convicted her of second-degree murder. She has served eight years of a fifteen-year sentence. She refused to participate in counseling programs because she claimed that she was not guilty of the crime for which she was convicted. During imprisonment she received citations for a series of minor infractions, such as stealing food from the cafeteria, refusing to obey instructions from corrections officers, and fighting with other inmates. Her mother, who was caring for her ten-year old daughter while she was prison, has recently died of cancer and the child has been placed in foster care. She has been promised a job working at a dry cleaning store.

20. **Probation:** If you were a judge, what kinds of offenders would you put on probation?

What kinds of offenders would you not place on probation?

If you were a probation officer, which aspect of your job would receive your strongest emphasis: surveillance/rule enforcement or social services/counseling to help reintegration? Why?

If you were a judge, what conditions/restrictions would you impose on probationers? Why?

21. **Intermediate Sanctions:** Take the following intermediate sanctions and list them in order of the sanctions that you believe are most effective (1 for most effective and 8 for least effective). (Corrections)

    For each one, describe its strengths and weaknesses with respect to the goals that should be accomplished:

    a. Fines
    b. Restitution
    c. Boot camps
    d. Intensive probation supervision
    e. Forfeiture
    f. Day reporting centers
    g. Community service
    h. Home confinement

22. Have the students debate whether ex-felons should be given the **right to vote**. (Corrections, Incarceration and Prison Society)

23. Have students design and administer a short questionnaire regarding opinions on the **use of intermediate sanctions**. The questions can be a "favor-oppose" format paring specific sanctions with specific crimes. Have the class discuss the results and implications of their findings. (Punishment and Sentencing)

24. Have the class collect literature on **the legal system and corrections**. Invite a correctional official to discuss the impact the courts have had on the state's correctional system. Allow students to question and raise issues identified in the literature with the official. Highlight how the opinions of the state official are similar or dissimilar to thoughts and ideas raised in the chapter. Have the students note the distinctions.

25. Develop an in-class debate that will discuss the **effectiveness of probation** as well as the future of the practice.

26. Collect information on the **organization of probation services** in your state. Have the students analyze the organization and comment on the advantages and disadvantages of such a structure in the delivery of probation services.

27. Invite a local judge to class to discuss the importance of **the pre-sentence investigation report** on sentencing. Have the judge comment on what weight is given to the report among his/her fellow judges. In addition, have the judge discuss the future role of pre-sentence investigation reports in the local judiciary. (Punishment and Sentencing)

28. Invite a **probation officer** to class to explain the realities of her or his job. How effective do they feel probation is? Is their outlook community justice, rehabilitation, retribution, or a different perspective?

29. Invite a local judge to class to discuss how that judge uses **intermediate sanctions** to widen the range of punishments available in his/her jurisdiction.

30. Have a correctional client from each of the **intermediate sanction programs in the area** visit the class to explain the program, the client's responsibilities, and the program's effects on the individual and his family.

31. Visit the local community corrections office. Discuss with the director the **goals and purposes of community corrections** in the state.

32. Have students collect newspaper clippings on **intermediate sanctions and community corrections** in the news. Have students comment on the image of community corrections portrayed by the newspapers and compare that with what is presented in the chapter.

33. Contact a local community corrections center where **parolees** reside. If possible, have the parolees discuss the role of prisoner economies in prison. Have them explain the working of the **prison economy**, and more importantly, the advantages and disadvantages of such a system.

34. Visit a local **community corrections center for women**. Discuss with the women the problems they are having in adjusting and what they think can be done to alleviate them. (Women)

35. Contact the office of public information in your state capital and request a copy of the state budget that outlines the amount of **money spent on corrections for men and women**. Is there a difference? Is the difference proportionate to the number of men and women incarcerated? (Women)

36. Ask students to list the **advantages and disadvantages of parole**. Compare the students' lists with the realities of parole mentioned in the chapter. Discuss with students how their perceptions are either congruent or incongruent with what is known about parole functioning.

37. If possible, have students attend **parole board hearings** for one week documenting both the reasons why prisons were denied parole and granted parole. Have the students write an essay stating their perceptions of the parole hearing process as they relate to specific correctional goals mentioned in the book.

38. Develop a scenario for **parole decision making**. Have the students decide if they would allow parole for a murderer who has served one-third of his sentence, with an excellent institutional record. Do the same with a drug offender with a poor institutional record. Ask, "Why did you grant or deny parole? What are some factors that make the parole decision so difficult?"

39. Invite a parolee to class to discuss **the experience of being on parole**. Have the students explore with him the problems he has with adjusting to the community and how he deals with them.

40. Invite an officer of the local probation department to class to demonstrate and discuss the use of **electronic monitoring**. Have students consider the capabilities and limits of technology.

41. Have a **probation officer and an intensive probation officer** discuss their roles and responsibilities. Compare their caseloads, degree of authority, level of intensity, and use of surveillance and control technologies.

42. Although we have witnessed a decrease in the rates of many crimes in recent years, currently we are at an all-time high in the number of people under some form of correctional supervision. Have students discuss how this can be so. One obvious answer is that we have a **wider variety of supervision options** available to us today than in the past. (Criminology)

43. To some, **probation** is seen as merely a "slap on the wrist." Have the students discuss which criminal incidents are best served by probation and which are not.

44. Invite a local **juvenile probation officer** to address your class regarding factors he or she considers when making a decision to violate a probationer. (Race)

45. Invite a juvenile probation officer to class to discuss **juvenile probation trends** in your locality. (Juvenile Justice)

46. Have the students develop a **juvenile probation plan** for a juvenile who has committed one of the following crimes...

   a. Possession with intent to deliver crack cocaine
   b. Burglary of an automobile
   c. Aggravated assault on a 70-year old lady
   d. Vandalism
   e. Shoplifting
   f. Pick pocketing
   g. Or any other offense.

Assume that the juvenile in question has no past criminal record. (Juvenile Justice)

### Incarceration and Prison Society

1. Arrange a class tour of your **local jail**. Prior to the tour, invite your local sheriff, or a correctional officer from the jail, to come to class to discuss issues faced by both the inmates and the sheriff's department.

2. Arrange for class tours of **minimum-, medium-, and maximum-security prisons**.

3. Divide students into small groups and have them design an **"ideal" prison**.

4. Encourage student discussion of **supermax prisons**.

5. Assign students to see what they can find out about **private boot camps** on the Internet.

6. Develop a research paper on the topic of issues faced by **jails**.

7. See if you can arrange for an ex-con to come to class and discuss **prison life**.

8. **Exercise: Prison education**

   Invite a teacher to class who teaches in a prison to discuss the types of classes offered for inmates.

9. Invite a **psychologist, or social worker**, who works with inmates to come to class to discuss their jobs.

10. Find out the **qualifications required for correctional officers** at the nearest prison. Have the students discuss their qualifications. Encourage student discussion of this occupation. Do any of them want to be a prison guard? Why or why not? ( Careers)

11. Encourage a discussion focusing on **prisoners' rights**. Do students think that prisoners have too many rights? (Criminal Law)

12. Invite a **parole officer** to come to class to discuss his or her job duties. See if it is possible for her or her to bring a parolee along. (Careers)

13. Divide the class into small groups. Have them discuss qualifications for the **"ideal" parole board member**.

14. Have students interview guards in a jail or prison and develop a paper on **guarding the institution** based on these interviews. (Careers)

15. Develop a research paper on the issues faced by **female inmates**.

16. Select two **prisoners' rights** and write a paper on these rights. (Criminal Law)

17. Arrange a class tour of a **juvenile detention facility or a training school**. (Juvenile Justice)

18. Visit the jail or prison as a group (with permission). Talk with administrators and staff about **prison goals and conditions**.

19. How often did **your state's corrections system** make the news over the past four years? What were the issues?

20. How do the **conditions in your state's prisons** match those of the movies?

21. Visit and interview a **parole officer** and discuss the questions raised in this chapter.

22. What are the **conditions of parole in your state**? Where are they published?

23. It has been stated that **rehabilitation** is almost impossible in the abnormal world of the prison. In your opinion is it possible or not to develop normal, positively productive citizens in the prisons of today? Please give your opinion and provide two constructive suggestions which might help this situation in a 1,500 word essay and cite the sources for all data used. (Corrections)

24. Divide the class into small groups. The students are consultants for a state department of corrections. The state needs to build a new prison because of **overcrowding** at its aging correctional institutions.

    The consultants' task is to design a new prison, including the physical layout of the building(s), plans for living space for the prisoners, and plans for programs and facilities. In designing the prison, the students need to consider a number of objectives:

    a. Making the facility safe and secure without employing an excessive number of staff personnel or otherwise producing excessive costs.

    b. Creating living conditions that meet constitutional standards for avoiding overcrowding and that create an environment that can be stable and controlled.

c.  Planning programs and facilities to achieve correctional goals. Because the state officials show great deference to the expert consultants, the consultants should also discuss and specify which goals (e.g., rehabilitation, incapacitation, retribution, etc.) their programs and facilities are intended to achieve.

After each group is finished, the entire class can compare the plans produced by each group. The exercise is intended to make students think seriously about the challenges that face corrections officials who must attempt to strike the appropriate balance between a variety of objectives: safety, security, staff morale, constitutional standards, rehabilitation, punishment, etc. (Corrections)

25. Debate the following question:

Has the correctional system within the United States become a **prison commercial complex**? Have a small group of students research this question from the perspective of corporations using government officials in order to profit from the "tough on crime" policies and have a separate group of students research the issue from the perspective of the prison system getting larger simply because the space is needed and must be developed due to the increased rate of incarceration. (Corrections, Community Corrections and Probation)

26. Discuss the **legacy of prisons**. What were prisons like in the 1940s and 1950s? 1960s and early 1970s? What has occurred in the last thirty years in the prison environment? (Corrections)

27  Discuss the **goals of incarceration**. Which is most important? Why? (Corrections)

28.  For this exercise, students can be divided into small groups or the problem can be discussed as an entire class. Tell the students to imagine that they are members of an advisory committee that must quickly advise a new warden on steps to take to prevent a **gang war**.

The warden is responsible for a new maximum security prison that is about to open. It is known that inmates being transferred to the prison include members of various gangs that have clashed in other institutions. There is a Mexican-American gang, an African-American gang, and a white gang. The new prison will also receive many of the state's youngest prisoners (ages 17-21) who were convicted for acts of violence. What steps should the warden take to minimize the prospects for violence? (Corrections)

29. **Prisons and their Purposes:** If you were in charge of a state corrections department, how would you design your prisons? For each question, assume that the prisons have one primary purpose (listed below) and describe the physical design, policies, and programs that you would implement to help the institution advance the overriding goal. ? (Corrections)

   a.  Custodial Model
   b.  Rehabilitation Model
   c.  Reintegration Model

30. Exercise: **Prisoners' Rights: You are the Judge**

Corrections officers at the main gate receive a report that a fight involving twelve prisoners has broken out in Cellblock C and that the corrections officers in Cellblock C are unable to break up the fight. Seven corrections officers run down the corridor from the main gate toward Cellblock C. As they round a corner, they practically run into inmate Joe Cottrell who is mopping and waxing the corridor floor. One officer grabs Cottrell by the shoulders and throws him aside while saying, "Get out of the way!" Cottrell falls into a wall, dislocates his shoulder, and later files a lawsuit against the officer by claiming that the rough treatment and resulting injury violated his Eighth Amendment right against cruel and unusual punishment. Were his Eighth Amendment rights violated? Explain.

A prison chapel is used every Sunday for Christian services. A small group of prisoners reserve the chapel for each Tuesday evening where they meet to study an ancient religion from Asia that they claim to follow. For two years, they use the chapel every Tuesday to meditate and discuss books about their religion, and they do not cause any trouble. Then, one year, Christmas falls on a Wednesday, and the Asian religion group is told that they cannot have their meeting because the chapel is needed for a Christian Christmas eve service. They file a lawsuit claiming that their First Amendment right to free exercise of religion is being violated because they cannot use the chapel on Christmas Eve. Are their rights being violated? Explain. (Corrections)

31. Debate the problem of **prisoners with HIV/AIDS**. Should prisoners be tested regularly and isolated because they might infect other prisoners? (Corrections)

32. Take the students on a field trip to a **men's prison and a woman's prison**. Students should reflect on these experiences by comparing and contrasting the two types of prisons. (Corrections)

33. Have the students create proposals that could be used to ease the **transition of a parolee** from prison to society.

34. Have the students debate whether ex-felons should be given the **right to vote**. (Corrections, Community Corrections and Probation)

35. **Prison Programs:** You are in charge of developing programs at a new prison. For each category of possible programs discuss whether you will recommend such programs for your prison. Why? If so, describe the goals and details of those programs.

    a. Educational Programs
    b. Vocational Programs
    c. Prison Industries
    d. Rehabilitative Programs

36. **Prison Problems:** If you were a prison warden, name three things that you would do to address each of the following issues. How effective do you think your strategies would be?

    a. Racial tensions between groups of inmates

    b. Prison gangs controlling the internal economy

    c. Mothers of small children serving long sentences in an isolated institution

37. Visit a **state prison** and have students write a reaction essay about their impressions of the types of people they observed. If possible, have students discuss with a staff person the problems found among the inmate population.

38. Contact a local community corrections agency to see if a meeting can be arranged with a former prisoner. Allow students the opportunity to ask the ex-offender about the **positive and negative aspects of prison treatment programs**.

39. Invite a psychologist who works with offenders to speak to the class about the issues on **mental illness, diagnosis, classification, and treatment of offenders**. If possible, have the psychologist explain the Diagnostic and Statistical Manual.

40. Have the students discuss potential options for dealing with **inmates who have contracted the HIV virus**. What method of housing these inmates would the students support? Why? If the students argue that the inmate with AIDS should be released, how does their solution comport with the various goals of punishment (i.e., rehabilitation, deterrence, retribution, and incapacitation).

41. Divide your class into groups and have the groups develop their own **prisoner classification system**, including specific criteria, with housing, work, educational and activity consequences clearly spelled out. Once developed, give each group a series of short "case files" of inmates who are to be classified and accordingly treated. In class, compare the consequences of their decisions and their classification systems.

42. Contact a local vendor of correctional services to discuss the advantages and disadvantages of **privatization** Have the students write an essay on what they thought were the most compelling arguments in the presentation. Read some essays in class to promote discussion of the issues. (Corrections)

43. Have a former prisoner discuss the **effects of incarceration**, specifically how overcrowding affects relations in prisons. Let students compare the speaker's ideas with those in the chapter.

44. Visit a state prison and if possible observe the **socialization patterns of prisoners**. Have students document what they believe are the major forms of socialization among prisoners. Finally, have students write an essay on what behaviors they observed and how those behaviors tie to a specific model of **inmate society** discussed in the chapter.

45. Invite a warden to class to examine the topic of **prison violence**. Have the students mention the alternatives explored in the chapter to reduce prison violence. See if the warden agrees or disagrees with these ideas.

46. If possible, invite an ex-convict to speak to the class and explain the **realities of prison life**. Is the life the speaker describes similar to that described in the book? Which is more indicative of the reality of prison life?

47. Assign your students a state of the union. Have each go to the web site of the **state prison / corrections system in that state**. Have them prepare an essay describing the system, its facilities, stated programs, and population make up including information about population demographics, age of facilities, and anything else of interest to the student. Then, hold a class discussion regarding their findings before collecting the essays. Encourage your students to print out pages of particular interest.

48. Arrange a tour of a **women's prison**. Have the students discuss with the staff the differences they think are present between women's prison and men's prisons. Finally, require the students to write an essay that highlights these differences. (Women)

49. Have the director of corrections in the state come to class and discuss the purpose of **female prisons**. Examine how programming is different for women when compared to men. Have the class explore the justifications for these differences with the director. (Women)

50. Arrange a visit to a **state prison facility**. Have the students discuss openly with correctional officers the problems they have with the structure of the prison. Subsequent to the visit require students to write an essay proposing solutions to the problems raised by the correctional officers.

51. Construct a debate format among students with opposing sides on the following issues. (Corrections)

   a.  **Prison Compliance Mechanisms** – Coercive vs. Normative — (How should we encourage compliance?)

b. **Prison Correctional Officer Positions** – Men vs. Women — (Who should govern inmates?)

52. Divide the class into **managerial and line personnel**. Have each group decide what their number one priority for the institution should be and put those beliefs into a credo. How are the credos similar? How are they different?

53. Contact the division of corrections in your state and obtain a list of **programs available within the prisons**. Have students debate which programs are the most beneficial to both the prisoner and society. (Corrections)

54. Visit a prison and discuss with a group of prisoners the role of **prison programming** in their lives. Explore the positive and negative aspects of programming in the prison.

55. Have the person in charge of **prison programming** in the state come to class to explain the degree, types, and purposes of programming in the prison system.

56. Set up an in-class debate format that will address the question: "Should we provide inmates with **free services while in prison?**"

57. Have a correctional counselor come to class to discuss the problems associated with counseling **the resistant inmate client**.

58. Divide the class into two groups: one that supports **the increase in incarceration** and one that does not. Have them debate their positions using the knowledge that they have gained so far in the course.

59. Have the students go to their state's department of correction website. Have them gather information as to the **race of the inmates** currently incarcerated. Have them discuss their views on why there are so many minorities incarcerated. (Race, Punishment and Sentencing)

60. Invite a prison administrator from a prison with a death row to discuss his/her views on **capital punishment**. Review your state's policies for carrying out an execution. (Punishment and Sentencing)

173

61. Arrange an individual or class **tour of a prison** if there is one in the area. Try to arrange some interviews with the warden, some prisoners, rehabilitative staff and custodial officers.

Possible discussion points: How many of the prisoners are engaged in work or programs and how many spend most of their time watching TV, listening to the radio, playing cards, lifting weights, etc.? Do you think that rehabilitation is possible for most prisoners in this environment? What is the attitude of the staff toward rehabilitation? What is the attitude of prisoners toward rehabilitation?

62. Divide students into groups and have each investigate a different prison in your state (for example, maximum and minimum security facilities, male and female facilities, facilities for adults and juveniles, etc.). Then, have the students present their findings in class in order to demonstrate the **range of facilities** available.

# CHAPTER 7

# JUVENILE JUSTICE, GANGS, AND DRUGS

## Juvenile Justice

1. Invite a police officer to class who is part of a gang unit, or juvenile squad, to discuss the issue of **juvenile delinquency** in your area. (Gangs)

2. Invite a judge to class who deals with juvenile cases. Have him or her discuss the various stages of the **juvenile justice process**. (Courts)

3. Find out what the statutes are in your state concerning **waiver to adult court**. Discuss these with the class. How do they feel about the issue of trying juveniles as adults? At what age do they think juveniles should be tried as adults? (Courts, Criminal Law)

4. What is student reaction to the **teen court** concept?

5. Invite a **juvenile probation officer** to come to class and discuss his or her job duties. Also have the probation officer discuss internship opportunities available for your students. (Community Corrections and Probation, Careers)

6. Arrange a class tour of a **juvenile detention facility** or a training school. (Incarceration and Prison Society)

7. Develop a research paper on the **child-saving movement** and it impact on juvenile justice.

8. Interview a Juvenile Court Judge. Develop a research paper on the pros and cons of **abolishing the juvenile court**.

9. According to your state statistics, **how many juvenile are under state supervision** in institutions, in probation, or in other programs? Provide a summary for your classmates and discuss.

10. Discuss the chapter material with a **juvenile officer** in the local police department. Does the interviewee accept the system as it is? Are there suggestions for improvement? What are the problems? (Policing)

11. Discuss the chapter material with an attorney who practices **juvenile law**. Does the interviewee accept the system as it is? Are there suggestions for improvement? What are the problems? (Criminal Law)

12. From the beginning of the nation, we have argued about how punitive we can be with children. The **ages of responsibility** are constantly adjusted to reflect the times and the juvenile court has been implemented. Still the debate continues. How much responsibility are we going to attribute to children of what age? (You know there are "adults" who are very irresponsible.) Focusing solely on responsibility, please justify your opinion in a 1,500 word essay using data and cite the sources for all data used. (Criminal Law)

13. Ask the class to discuss the question **"Should juveniles receive the death penalty for murder"**? As the students explore the question, their attention should be directed to the philosophical underpinnings of juvenile justice which dictate that juvenile offenders should be treated differently than adults with respect to culpability and punishment.

    In particular, competing goals of retribution, incapacitation, deterrence, and rehabilitation come into sharp focus when considering which objectives are arguably advanced by executing or not executing juvenile murderers. Should there be a cut-off age for juvenile's eligibility for the death penalty? If a nine year old intentionally takes his parents' gun and shoots another child because of a dispute over baseball cards, should that child be subject to the death penalty? Is there any specific age that is too young to be subject to the death penalty? Does it depend on the heinousness of the crime or upon the characteristics of an individual child? Finally, if children can be subject to the death penalty, then is there any reason to treat children differently than adults by having a separate juvenile justice system? (Criminal Law)

14. Have the students debate whether a person under eighteen years of age should be **tried as an adult**. What types of crime would require a juvenile to be tried in adult court? (Criminal Law)

15. **Treatment of Delinquents:** Assume each of the following occupational roles. In each role, formulate a recommendation for what should happen to a fourteen-year-old boy whose seventeen-year-old companion killed a man while the two of them attempted to steal a bicycle.

    a. Social Worker
    b. State Legislator
    c. Director of Group Home for Delinquents
    d. Juvenile Court Judge

16. Have students research either **bullying or school violence**. Ask students to outline their findings and to be prepared to share them with the class.

17. What **programs for youths** are available in your community? Your school system?

18. Have a juvenile probation officer, prosecutor, and/or guardian ad litem/defense attorney come and speak to the class about the **special problems in dealing with juveniles in the criminal justice system**. (Corrections)

19. Find out what the statues are in your state concerning **waiver to adult court**. Discuss these with the class. How do they feel about the issue of trying juveniles as adults? At what age do they think that juveniles should be tried as adults?

20. Ask your students based on the current attitudes toward juvenile offenders, what do they predict **juvenile corrections** will look like 20 years from now?

21. What are the **maximum and minimum ages for juvenile court jurisdiction for delinquent acts** in the state where you reside or attend college? Do you think these ages are too high or too low? What services does your state provide for children who commit crimes while under the minimum age of juvenile court jurisdiction? (Courts)

    Possible discussion points: Most states do not provide juvenile court jurisdiction for those who reach eighteen. In Texas, juvenile court jurisdiction is not available for those who are seventeen. If

177

the child is below juvenile court jurisdiction, the primary options are mental health, or some form of neglect/dependency proceeding.

22. What social trends will likely have an impact on **juvenile crime and juvenile courts** in the next few decades? How will the system respond to these changes? (Courts)

    Possible discussion points: Demographic changes such as the number of people in the crime-prone teen years will be important. As senior citizens become an increasing proportion of the population, they will compete with the children of the poor for government assistance.

23. In his book *The Child Savers*, Anthony Platt suggests that **juvenile justice reforms** were motivated more by class interest and prejudice than a sincere desire to help children. Do you agree or disagree?

    Possible discussion points: This may or may not be true. Weren't the children of the poor and immigrants the main targets of the Child Savers? On the other hand, weren't these also the children most in need of help?

24. Discuss the theory of ***parens patriae*** and its importance in juvenile court. Be sure to provide examples.

    Some main points: By the end of the 1800s, the conception of children as miniature adults was fading. Children were seen as persons with less than fully developed moral and cognitive capacities. This shift in thinking was reflected in the legal doctrine of *parens patriae* (state as parent). No longer were parents considered to have sole and exclusive legal responsibility over their children. If the parents failed in their responsibility to raise a child properly, the state could intervene to protect the child's welfare. In extreme circumstances parental rights over their children could be terminated altogether

25. Discuss the **Progressive and Child Saver movements** and their impact on juvenile justice.

    Some main points: Juvenile courts began in the late nineteenth century. The major economic and social changes of the late nineteenth century prompted a rethinking of the role of youth. The

178

result was the creation of specialized courts to deal with what were thought to be distinctly youth-oriented problems.

Beginning around 1890, members of the Progressive movement advocated a variety of political, economic, and social reforms. They were genuinely concerned about the economic disparities, social disorders, and excesses of industrialization, particularly as they affected children. Among their concerns was the plight of poor, urban youth. One part of the Progressive movement was termed the "Child Savers." This group of elite and middle-class reformers pushed for creation of special courts to help, rather than punish, juveniles.

26. Define, discuss, compare, and contrast the **crime control (conservative) and due process (liberal) approaches to juvenile justice**. Be sure to provide examples.

    Some main points: The debate is generally between the conservatives who advocate a crime control model stressing punishment, and liberals who advocate prevention and treatment.

27. Discuss and describe the **main procedural points on a juvenile case**.

    Some main points: The steps in a typical juvenile case are as follows:

    a. Delinquency (Crime)
    b. Summons (Arrest)
    c. Intake (Initial Hearing)
    d. Detention Hearing
    e. Petition
    f. Conference
    g. Evidence gathering and suppressing
    h. Plea Bargaining
    i. Adjudicatory Hearing
    j. Disposition (sentencing)
    k. Appeal.

28. In the jurisdiction where you live or go to college, **what is the age at which persons are deemed to be adults and thus are tried in adult court rather than juvenile court?** Is this age too low or too high? Do juveniles take advantage of the system? (Courts)

Some Discussion Points: Juveniles are probably less deterrable and more rehabilitatable than most adults. This would seem to indicate that juvenile court would be better for them and society. In Texas, persons are not eligible for juvenile court for any crime committed after they turn seventeen.

29. What is the rationale behind **DARE programs**? (Policing)

30. Have the students look up the **legal definition of juvenile delinquency** in your state.

31. Have your students read the government section of the phone book to find all of the **social service agencies that deal with juveniles**.

32. Have your students fill out an anonymous self-report survey indicating how much **juvenile delinquency** the class has committed.

33. Have your students bring in some of the most violence rap and gangster rap that they own. Discuss the **effects of this music on the juvenile delinquency**.

34. Introduce your students to the FBI website and have them explore the **statistics on juvenile crime**.

35. Have the students compare **current juvenile murder rates** with murders rates in the '50s and '60s.

36. Invite members of the **Big Brother and Big Sister organization** to attend your class and discuss how a teenager's life can be changed by intervention at a critical turning point.

37. Invite the Boy Scouts and Girl Scouts of America to your class to discuss what options children have besides joining a **gang**. (Gangs)

38. Contact your local police department and have your gang officer come out and discuss **what type of gangs you have in your city**. (Gangs)

39. Arrange to have the class visit a **local jail** and observe if there is a separation of males and females and boys and girls. (Women)

40. Invite a Department of Human Services representative to your class to discuss what criteria they use and how they **remove a battered child from the home**.

41. Invite a **guardian ad litem** to discuss with the class what his/her role is in the court process

42. Assign the class to go to the mall and sit and observe **gang members**; their colors and the way they dress. (Gangs)

43. Invite the **local police department gang intervention unit** to speak to your class. (Gangs)

44. Have your students contact your local school districts and obtain their policies on **school discipline**. Discuss if their policies are consistent with Supreme Court decisions on the issue.

45. Have a juvenile court lawyer visit the class to take about **juvenile rights**. (Courts)

46. Do a survey of all of your Criminal Justice majors in the department and see if they say that **drugs and weapons were prevalent in their high schools**. (Drugs)

47. Have the local DARE officer come in to discuss the **DARE program in your community**. (Policing, Drugs)

48. Look at the types of **prevention of delinquency** in the teen years. Which ones are most effective at curbing juvenile delinquency? Discuss the programs that are available in your area.

49. How do you see the future of the **prevention of delinquency programs**? What can be done to convince others that they are effective?

50. Assign the students Anthony Platt's work *The Child Savers*. Discuss the work in detail.

51. Have the students visit the juvenile court in your jurisdiction. Have them interview the juvenile court judge, prosecutor, or a defense attorney who does a lot of work in juvenile court. Have them write a report on **how the juvenile justice system functions in your locality**. (Courts)

52. Take the class on a tour of the **juvenile detention facility** in your locality. (Corrections)

53. Have the local **Community Policing Officer** come talk to your class about what the police department is doing to help juveniles. (Policing)

54. **Juvenile Executions:** The U.S. is one of the few countries in the world that allow juveniles to be executed. Have the students go to...

   http://www.deathpenaltyinfo.org/article.php?scid=27&did=203#ag eregs

   Have the students examine the data at this site. Then discuss the findings with the class.

55. Bring in a juvenile court judge or an attorney who practices in juvenile court and have them explain the **workings of the juvenile justice system in your community**.

56. In addition to delinquency in the juvenile court, there is another aspect of the juvenile court system: **Children who are involved in the juvenile court system because of neglect or abuse by the parents or caregivers.** Discuss this part of the juvenile court system with the class. Note: inviting a juvenile defense attorney may be useful in this activity.

57 Invite a juvenile probation officer to class to discuss **juvenile probation trends in your locality**. (Community Corrections and Probation)

58. Have the students develop **a juvenile probation plan** for a juvenile who has committed one of the following crimes...

   a. Possession with intent to deliver crack cocaine
   b. Burglary of an automobile
   c. Aggravated assault on a 70-year old lady
   d. Vandalism
   e. Shoplifting
   f. Pick pocketing
   g. Or any other offense.

   Assume that the juvenile in question has no past criminal record. (Community Corrections and Probation)

59. Have the class construct a letter to **INTERPOL** requesting crime data on **juvenile street gangs and/or other juvenile crime problems.**

60. Go to the website of the National Gang Crime Research at www.ngcrc.com and see what information can be gleaned on **international-type gangs.**

61. Ask one of the school's Sociologists, who is a demographer, to discuss the **effects of juvenile population growth on the juvenile crime rate.**

62. Discuss whether America will use **more incarceration or more treatment of juvenile offenders in the future.**

## Gangs

1. Write a research paper on the impact of gangs on **crime and victimization trends.** (Victimization)

2. Invite a police officer to class who is part of a gang unit, or juvenile squad, to discuss the issue of **juvenile delinquency** in your area. (Juvenile Justice)

3. Were **gangs present in your high school**? How did you know? If they were, did they present a threat?

4. Are there efforts in your community to **combat the gang problem**?

5. **Injunctions against gangs** have been a highly successful strategy in some cities and states. Have students research the controversy surrounding the constitutionality of using injunctions in this way. Ask students to be prepared to share their findings with the class.

6. The city of Boston, using community policing strategies, won an Innovations in American Government Award for its Operation Cease Fire. Have students research this much-replicated program and explain why it was considered innovative and how it affected **gang violence and teenage deaths by handguns.**

7. Use the **GangsOrUs website** (www.gangsorus.com) and outline the information given for gangs in your state.

8. Research what **gang control strategies** are used in your community to address the gang problem.

9. What types of **criminal and civil laws** have been used to try to deal with gang problems? (Criminal Law)

   Some main points: A number of state and city governments have passed criminal laws to regulate gang behavior. In some places, it's a crime to participate in a gang. Some statutes and ordinances have stiffened the penalties for crimes committed by gang members. Others make it a crime to encourage minors to participate in gangs. Some have applied organized crime statutes to gangs. A few have punished parents for their children's gang activities. Cities have also passed ordinances banning gang members from certain public places, particularly city parks.

   In addition to criminal penalties, cities have also turned to civil remedies to control gang activity. For example, in the ancient civil remedy injunction to abate public nuisances, which is still used, government attorneys ask courts to declare gang activities and gang members public nuisances and to issue injunctions (court orders) to abate (stop) the public nuisance.

10. Have students go to the **Office of Juvenile Justice Delinquency Prevention's Gang Prevention Programs** website at...

    http://www.dsgonline.com/mpg2.5/gang_prevention.htm

    Ask the students to review the information and provide a written report describing the steps they would take to coordinate the law enforcement response and investigations in their community with the services and programs mentioned on the site. (Criminal Investigation)

11. A small juvenile gang composed of no more than 15 members has been active in the community recently. Their members have been linked to drug sales, assaults, thefts and graffiti. The gang is multi-racial and appears to be led by a slightly older person, who is about 20 years of age. What approach would you take to **reduce or eliminate these gang problems**? (Criminal Investigation)

12. Invite the **Boy Scouts and Girl Scouts of America** to your class to discuss what options children have besides joining a gang. (Juvenile Justice)

13. Contact your local police department and have your gang officer come out and discuss **what type of gangs you have in your city**. (Juvenile Justice)

14. Invite the local jail administrator to speak to your class about any **gang problems that they may be having in your county jail**.

15. Assign the class to go to the mall and sit and observe **gang members; their colors and the way they dress**. (Juvenile Justice)

16. Invite the **local police department gang intervention unit** to speak to your class. (Juvenile Justice)

### Drugs

1. Invite a DEA agent to class to discuss the **role of the DEA in controlling the drug trade**. (Careers)

2. Arrange for the class to sit in on hearings in a specialty court, such as a **drug court**. (Courts)

3. Identify using the DEA's charts (either from a speaker or from Internet research) the **major drugs of abuse in the U.S.** and the extent and amount of abuse.

4. Visit the spokesman for the **local drug unit from the police department**. Discuss his or her views of the drug problem and compare them to your views. (Policing)

5. The **"drug war"** apparently needs help. Assuming you want to help the national effort on drug control (not necessarily "war"), what package of three policy changes would you recommend?

6. Debate whether the War on Drugs contributes to the **racism** in society. Is the criminal justice system racist? How? (Criminal Justice)

7. What do you see as the relationship between drugs and the **American Dream**? Crime, drugs and the American Dream are

integrally related. In fact a drug problem may be the result of the American Dream for many people.

8. What **programs in your community** are directed at the drug problem? Have you participated in any of them?

9. Did you receive **DARE training** as a child? What were your impressions? Do you believe it had any effect on your attitudes and actions regarding drugs?

10. What are the three core principles of the **National Drug Control Strategy**? Which do you believe to be the most effective? The least? The three core principles are...

   a. stopping drug use before it starts: education and community action

   b. healing America's drug users: getting treatment resources where they are needed

   c. disrupting the market: attacking the economic basis of the drug trade

11. What bar marketing promotions are you aware of that encourage **irresponsible drinking**?

12. Research what colleges or universities in your area have **programs addressing student alcohol use and misuse**. Are they effective?

13. Conduct a survey on your campus of **student drinking behaviors**. Include binge drinking and drinking and driving.

14. The War on Drugs has led to many changes in the judicial system, notably **drug courts**. Are drug courts effective? Is the use of **therapeutic jurisprudence** an effective philosophy for dealing with this problem? Is there a better solution?

   Possible discussion points: Sanctions for the war on drugs have ranged from asset forfeiture and prison time to treatment-oriented ideals like therapeutic jurisprudence (range of punishments). Treatment oriented efforts seem to be effective for first time offenders. With the broad range of cases, no one solution will fit all.

15. Ask students to visit the **Drug Enforcement Administration's website** (http://www.usdoj.gov/dea/) and review the recent major cases featured there.

    Have the students each provide a short written report in which they explain the primary focus of the operations as well as any commonalities they have been able to discern in terms of where the operations have developed, how the cases have been investigated, and what issues have been involved. (Criminal Investigation)

16. Divide the class into groups and ask them to discuss the following issues: (Criminal Investigation)

    a.  A highly organized group of **drug sellers** exists in your community. It is well-managed and efficient at evading authorities. Previous attempts to infiltrate the organization using undercover officers or informants have ended in failure, and in one case the officer was in grave danger. What other tactics might be in order?

    b.  **Drug sales** have increased dramatically at two local high schools. What actions can local law enforcement take to reduce this problem?

    c.  What actions might a law enforcement agency take that would combine both **enforcement and prevention of drug-related crime**?

17. Look at the statutes concerning various drugs. Have the class debate the issue of **legalizing** any or all types of drugs. Are the penalties currently in place appropriate? Why or why not? (Criminology)

18. Do a survey of all of your Criminal Justice majors in the department and see if they say that **drugs and weapons were prevalent in their high schools**. (Juvenile Justice)

19. Have the local DARE officer come in to discuss the **DARE program** in your community. (Juvenile Justice, Policing)

20. Have the students go to...

    http://www.usdoj.gov/dea/concern/concern.htm

This website provides for a detailed description of the various **illegal drugs that the DEA comes into contact with**. Have each student examine a different drug and give a brief presentation in class. Some examples of issues for the students to explore are: what effects and consequences the drug has on the user, who the typical user is, what the drug looks like, whether the drug comes in different forms, how the drug is introduced to the American market, how is the particular drug ingested, what the street name is for the drug, and how much the drug costs on the street.

21. Have the student examine **drug data for the different states**. Assign each student two states to compare and contrast the data. One of the sources for them to use is...

   http://www.usdoj.gov/dea/pubs/state_factsheets.html

   Have them write down their findings and then as a class, compare data.

# CHAPTER 8

# ETHICAL AND SOCIAL ISSUES

## Ethics

1. Interview members of the local police force and criminal court on the issues of ethics discussed in your text. Develop a paper on **ethics in law enforcement and criminal court**. (Criminal Justice)

2. Many police departments require that recruits be of "good moral character." This means that, to some extent, police officers are held to **a higher moral standard** than the average citizen. Encourage student discussion of this issue. (Policing)

3. Write a paper on the impact of **corruption on the area of policing**. (Policing)

4. Locate, distribute, and discuss **the ethics statement** of the local police or the sheriff. (Policing)

5. On one hand, we value local autonomy and accountability of our law enforcers – especially the sheriff whom we elect, but on the other hand all the rest of our law enforcers are appointed by other politicians who shield the enforcers from the public. This raises the question: How much **accountability** can we expect from our law enforcers and how do we insure we get such accountability? Please justify your opinion in a 1,500 word essay and cite the sources for all data used. (Policing)

6. Divide the class into small groups. Each group is to act as a committee within a state legislature. In the aftermath of the Rodney King case in 1992, in which police officers were convicted on federal civil rights charges after being videotaped while beating a motorist who had been speeding, citizens in your state have complained that there is inadequate control over police who use excessive force. These special legislative committees are assigned the task of recommending procedures and remedies to handle **citizens' complaints about the police**. The committee has four specific proposals to consider. They may recommend that the

legislature enact any or all of these proposals, or they can develop alternative proposals to recommend to the legislature. (Policing)

a.  Proposal #1: All counties, cities, and towns will be required to develop internal review boards within law enforcement agencies. These review boards will be composed of both senior officers and patrol officers. In response to complaints from citizens about specific officers, the boards will investigate the complaints and may take testimony from victims, witnesses, and police officers. The boards will issue findings and recommendations to the local police chief or county sheriff. If the findings are against the officer, the officer will have the opportunity to appeal to the local police chief or county sheriff before punishments, ranging from letter of reprimand to suspension to dismissal, are imposed by the police chief or sheriff.

b.  Proposal #2: All counties, cities, and towns will develop citizen review boards to evaluate complaints from citizens concerning law enforcement officers. The review boards will be comprised of citizens appointed by the local county, city, or town council. The review board will investigate citizen complaints and will take testimony from victims, witnesses, and police officers. The board will make findings and disciplinary recommendations to the local county, city, or town council. If the findings are against the law enforcement officer, the officer may appeal to the local county, city, or town council before the council imposes punishment.

c.  Proposal #3: The state legislature shall enact a law making law enforcement officers personally liable for damages caused by the excessive use of force. Plaintiffs must show by a preponderance of evidence that excessive force was used.

d.  Proposal #4: The state legislature shall enact a law making counties, cities, and towns liable for damages caused by their police officers' excessive use of force. Plaintiffs must show evidence beyond a reasonable doubt that excessive force was used.

In discussing these alternatives, the small groups should consider which constituencies will favor which proposals and the potential

190

consequences of each proposal. For example, will an internal review board favor police officers' accounts of events over the testimony by citizen witnesses? Should citizens, like police officers, have the opportunity to appeal the board's decisions if they disagree with them? Will a citizen review board attempt to interfere with police operations and policies in ways that police officers view as detrimental to their law enforcement functions? How will police officers respond to Proposal #3 in which a jury can potentially bankrupt them by second-guessing a judgment that they made in the heat of a stressful conflict situation during an arrest or other incident? Can any citizen meet the standard of proof required under Proposal #4 ("beyond a reasonable doubt") in order to receive compensation from the government? It is difficult to strike a careful balance between protecting police officers' discretionary judgments from undue second-guessing and preventing the use of excessive force.

7. Debate in class with the students the **best methods to hold police accountable**. Are there any alternatives that are not listed in the textbook? (Policing)

8. Have you witnessed police exercise their discretion? How did it impress you? Anyone who has received a traffic ticket or only a warning has experienced **police discretion**. (Policing)

9. **What decisions commonly made by police officers involve ethical considerations?** Answers will vary but could include truthfulness in court (especially when the accused might go free on a technicality) declining gifts, gratuities and "police discounts," how suspects in their custody will be treated. (Policing)

10. Which seems more "just" to you: **retributive justice or restorative justice**? (Policing)

11. Discuss the need to **balance judicial independence and judicial accountability**. Be sure to provide examples. (Courts)

   Some main points: The rationale for judicial independence is to protect judges and the judiciary from outside control and from fallout from unpopular decisions. However, procedures must also be in place to discipline or remove errant judges, as corrupt or wayward judges deface judicial integrity and the public's confidence in the judiciary. Therefore, a delicate balance must be struck in establishing procedures and systems to protect both the judiciary and the public.

12. In many American courts for years, **plea bargaining** was officially taboo. However, it was carried on and everyone involved denied that it existed. Although the defendant, defense attorney, prosecutor, and probably the judge knew there was a bargain, its existence was denied on the record. What does this practice say about the quality and ethics of the lawyers involved? (Courts)

Some main points: We expect courts to exemplify the highest ideals of truth, honor and justice, and yet they dishonored those ideals. It is no wonder that many people are cynical or distrustful about the criminal justice system.

13. You are confronted with the following **Dirty Harry Problem**. Your friend, Bill, became a police officer in your home town, the city of Bigproblems. During his academy training and field training, he was very happy about the job and constantly conveyed this to you. However, after his first month on patrol, as a community beat officer in a high crime public housing development, his personality seems to change. You begin to worry about him, and one night when you are out to dinner together, you ask him if anything has happened.

He confides in you that he had arrested a 20-year-old resident, Bigman Doper, for dealing drugs on his beat, several weeks ago, and had been disappointed that the court had sentenced him to probation, even though it was his second drug arrest.

You tell him that you understand his disappointment, but caution him to remember that the actions of courts are beyond his control and that he should just continue to do his job.

He then tells you that the court's decision was not his major concern. He relates that he had been complaining in the locker room about the court decision and had been approached by Hotshot Cassidy, a 20-year veteran of the department, who said, "Hey kid, don't worry about it, I'll fix Bigman for you." He then tells you that a week later he observed Bigman walking through the streets of the development and observed that he had been the victim of a vicious beating. Later at the station house Cassidy approached him and said, "You see what I did to Bigman, kid."

Bill asks your advice.

14. Define **police corruption** and give several examples of it.

15. What is **police misconduct**, other than corruption and brutality? Identify some of the forms it takes.

16. Because of your experience in taking this course, you have been appointed Assistant to the Police Commissioner of Anycity, USA. Anycity has had a ten-year tradition of numerous **brutality and corruption complaints** against its officers. The Commissioner requests your advice regarding the effects of these allegations and methods he can take to reduce them.

17. The peacemaking movement advocates for more "humanist solutions to crime." Break students into groups and have them brainstorm as to what these **humanist solutions** might look like. Remember that Pepinsky and Quinney advocate for mediation and conflict resolution policies. (Criminology)

18. Have the class watch the 1973 movie, *Serpico*. After the movie, break the class up into discussion groups. Ask the groups to discuss such topics as **the blue curtain subculture, ethics, Internal Affairs, and discretion**. (Policing)

19. Rank the following values in order of importance, with #1 representing the most important **value** to you, and so on. Now go through the list again and rank these values according to how you believe most people would rank them. Compare your answers with others as a class exercise and discuss how these values impact criminal justice professionals.

    a. Achievement
    b. Friendship
    c. Power
    d. Altruism
    e. Health
    f. Recognition
    g. Autonomy
    h. Honesty

i.   Religion
j.   Beauty
k.   Justice
l.   Success
m.   Creativity
n.   Knowledge
o.   Wealth
p.   Duty
q.   Love
r.   Wisdom
s.   Emotional well-being
t.   Loyalty
u.   Family Pleasure

20. Watch a movie or video of someone making an ethical decision
    and analyze their actions using the ethical pyramid to identify
    which **ethical system** they seem to be using.

### Ethical Pyramid

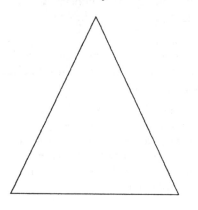

**Moral Judgment:** A woman who goes out drinking leaving her children at home is bad.

**Moral Rules:** Women should take care of their children. People drink to excess. Children should come before self. Drinking should be done in moderation. One should do one's duty.

**Ethical System:** This could be ethical formalism or utilitarianism or religion or ethics of care. The rules are logically inconsistent with egoism.

21. Have students work in groups and assign each group a different
    **ethical system** and then compare how they resolved an ethical
    dilemma.

22. Read *The Merchant of Venice* and discuss how Shakespeare views
    **justice**.

23. Have students do newspaper search of **restorative justice programs**.

24. Watch a video on mental illness and discuss what should be done with **offenders who are diagnosed with mental illness**.

25. Develop a **model ethics curriculum** for either law enforcement or corrections.

26. Have the class develop a **Code of Ethics** for police officers.

27. Have the students find statistics on police-stops to discuss **racial profiling** for your city or town.

28. Locate newspaper articles of current events involving your local police department and identify whether a **crime-control or public servant approach** can be identified.

29. Have students do informal research on local policies regarding **gratuities**.

30. Watch the video of the Rodney King beating and identify the aggressive moves that justified the **continued use of force**.

31. Have students conduct newspaper research of **ethical scandals in law enforcement.**

32. Watch the movie *Training Day* and identify how the **noble cause of drug interdiction** was corrupted.

33. Watch any movie wherein **an attorney is faced with an ethical dilemma(s)** and analyze the decision making using ethical systems.

34. Make a courtroom visit and develop a research project to explore the **misconduct of prosecutors** (the point of this exercise is to show how it is difficult to discover wrongdoing on the part of prosecutors).

35. Invite a defense attorney to class and have him or her explain how they can **"defend guilty people."**

36. Research any type of **judicial misconduct** – either through academic sources or newspaper sources.

37. Have the class debate **capital punishment** and then have them identify the arguments as to whether they are utilitarian or from some other ethical system.

38. Explore the concept of **just desert** by discussing what an appropriate sentence is for different types of offenders.

39. Watch a prison movie and identify any **ethical dilemmas of the correctional professionals.**

40. Do a newspaper search of any **correctional corruption scandals** in your state.

41. Read about the **Zimbardo experiment** and have a group discussion as to what conclusions one can draw from it about the influence of an incarcerative setting. (Research Methods)

42. Break the class into groups and have them resolve the following dilemmas of a probation officer using an **ethical system** (assign different groups different ethical systems).

   a.  I had a cousin on probation for his second DWI. No one in the family knows he is on probation. At a family gathering I see the probationer drinking (more than one drink).

   b.  A friend from high school had a boyfriend on probation. The boyfriend had violated his conditions of probation and an M.T.R.P. (Motion to Revoke Probation) was filed in his case. The girlfriend wanted me to give her confidential information out of his file.

   c.  I was having dinner at a nice restaurant and the manager on duty happened to be on my caseload and offered me a free dinner and gave me basketball tickets to five games.

   d.  I discovered that the applicant was an illegal alien but had a family of four with a baby who was born with a defect. His wife did not work and he was the sole provider of the family. The dilemma was that if INS was contacted, the individual would be deported while his family stayed with no support.

   e.  Do I not collect fees from a client who is a single mother with three children because it would come out of her budget and mean she must neglect the needs of her children, or do I

196

collect the fees and disregard the problems the client is struggling with, and alienate the client more?

43. Bring in **probation or parole officers** and have them discuss ethical issues that they have faced.

44. Create a survey of **sentencing options** that cover traditional and restorative justice options and survey an Intro class to determine if people are favorably inclined toward such sanctions.

45. Create a chart comparing **noble cause arguments in the drug war to noble cause arguments in the war on terror** – identify where you would see that the "end" justifies otherwise negative means.

46. Have the class research on what is happening to the Patriot Act; detentions of enemy combatants; wiretapping of citizens; and other tools of the **war on terror**.

47. Using your classroom computer, access the **New York City Civilian Complaint Review Board** website at...

    http://nyc.gov/html/ccrb

    Review various complaint cases and moderate a class discussion of the complaints and the responses of both the New York Police Department and the Civilian Complaint Review Board. (Race)

48. Invite the Chief of your local police department to address the class regarding the department's procedures for handling **civilian complaints**. (Race)

49. Have student role players act out an unscripted simulation of a **confrontation between a police officer and a citizen**. Set the scene, but don't tell the players what they should or should not do. (Except, of course, to ban physical contact!)

    Have the remainder of the class critique how each player contributed to the confrontational tension. Discuss actions the players might have taken to defuse the tension and achieve a more satisfactory result. (Race)

# Race

1. Would you favor eliminating the word *minority* when talking about **diversity**? If so, what term would you use instead?

2. Do you consider yourself **"culturally literate?"** Why or why not?

3. Have you encountered instances of **racism**? Explain.

4. **Diversity Terminology:** Have students research one of the following subjects and write a brief report of their findings:

   a. Discrimination
   b. Jargon
   c. Listening
   d. Nonverbal communication
   e. Prejudices
   f. Stereotypes

5. **Diversity Concepts:** Have students research and report on at least one of the following subjects:

   a. Cultural conflict
   b. Hate crime
   c. Homelessness
   d. Racial profiling
   e. Racism

6. Have the students go to their state's department of correction website. Have them gather information as to the **race of the inmates** currently incarcerated. Have them discuss their views on why there are so many minorities incarcerated. (Incarceration and Prison Society, Punishment and Sentencing)

7. Why have police departments historically had a poor relationship with the **African-American community**? (Policing)

8. Name and describe **some programs police departments have initiated between special populations of citizens**. Which one of them do you believe offers the best service to a special population group? (Policing)

9. Discuss the many **ways that African-Americans and women have been discriminated against in policing**. (Women)

10. Ask students to research 2000 census data and the latest UCR data for your city and your state. Discuss identified **racial and ethnic disparities** with particular attention given to data flaws identified in this chapter.

11. Poll the class to determine the extent of its **multiracial/multiethnic makeup.** Ask such students to relate difficulties they have encountered as a result of their backgrounds. Have them describe techniques they employ to overcome such difficulties.

12. **Diversity and the Media:** Have the students monitor local television news shows in your area for a two-week period and document...

    a. The number of crime stories presented, by category (violent vs. property)

    b. If identifiable, the race/ethnicity and gender of the offender

    c. If identifiable, the race/ethnicity and gender(s) of the victim(s).

    Moderate a discussion of the findings during class.

13. Ask the students to research **employment and income** data for your city categorized by race and ethnicity. Moderate a discussion of the findings during class.

14. Have the students access the U.S. Department of Commerce's Bureau of Economic Analysis web site and **examine state and local income data**. Moderate a class discussion about current and future growth trends by national region, particularly addressing why some regions are likely to grow while others indicate coming decline.

15. Using your classroom computer, access the **New York City Civilian Complaint Review Board** website at...

    http://nyc.gov/html/ccrb.

    Review various complaint cases and moderate a class discussion of the complaints and the responses of both the New York Police Department and the Civilian Complaint Review Board. (Ethics)

16. Invite the Chief of your local police department to address the class regarding the department's procedures for handling **civilian complaints**. (Ethics)

17. Have student role players act out an unscripted simulation of a **confrontation between a police officer and a citizen**. Set the scene, but don't tell the players what they should or should not do. (Except, of course, to ban physical contact!)

    Have the remainder of the class critique how each player contributed to the confrontational tension. Discuss actions the players might have taken to defuse the tension and achieve a more satisfactory result. (Ethics)

18. Show the movie "Gideon's Trumpet," about the landmark U.S. Supreme Court ruling in the case *Gideon v. Wainwright* (1963).

19. Invite a local prosecutor to address the class regarding factors used in his or her office when **making charge and plea bargaining decisions.** (Courts)

20. Tell your students they are the presiding judge hearing **first appearance bail applications**. From your local prosecutor, obtain redacted copies of genuine arrest reports used to present the state's case at initial appearances. Present each case and ask the students how they would rule regarding bail for the defendant. Have them explain their reasoning. (Courts)

21. Show the *Investigative Reports* documentary movie "The Farm: Life Inside Angola Prison Farm," which, in part, relates the compelling case of **Wilbert Rideau.**

22. Invite a local county court administrator to address the class regarding the **jury pool selection process** used in your county and the types of problems encountered. (Courts)

23. Moderate an in-class debate between a team of students presenting Professor Paul Butler's views on **racially based jury nullification,** and a second team presenting author Randall Kennedy's opposing views. (Courts)

24. African Americans are more likely than whites to be willing to serve time in prison rather than be sentenced to some alternative to incarceration such as electronic monitoring or intensive

200

supervision probation. What accounts for these **racial differences in perceptions of the severity of sanctions?**

25. Those who champion the **appointment/election of racial minorities to the bench** argue that African American and Hispanic judges could make a difference. Why? Does research comparing the sentencing decisions of white judges to those of African American or Hispanic judges confirm or refute this assumption?

26. Do you agree with the Supreme Court's decision upholding sentencing enhancements for **hate crimes**? Why or why not?

27. Moderate a class discussion on the **100-to-1 federal sentencing differential for possession of crack cocaine versus possession of powder cocaine.**

28. In *Gregg v. Georgia*, the Supreme Court assumed that racial discrimination would not be a problem under the guided-discretion statutes enacted in the wake of the *Furman* decision. Does the empirical evidence support or refute this assumption?

29. **Amnesty International** reports that 123 prisoners have been released in the U.S. since 1973 after evidence emerged of their innocence of the crimes for which they were sentenced to death. Have your students research these cases and present their findings to the class

30. Invite a local member of the ACLU to address the class regarding the **capital sentencing process and ongoing reform/abolition efforts**. (Punishment and Sentencing)

31. Moderate a class debate on **capital punishment**. (Punishment and Sentencing)

32. Do you think prison gang formation is influenced most by external forces and the **gang affiliations** offenders bring to prison from the street or by the internal forces of the prison environment, such as racial composition? What arguments can you offer to support your position?

33. Invite a parolee or probationer to address your class about daily **life under correctional supervision.**

34. There is a common perception that the typical **juvenile offender** is a person of color. Is this an accurate perception?

35. Why is there greater potential for racial discrimination in the **juvenile justice system** than in the adult justice system?

36. Studies of the juvenile justice system reveal that racial minorities are subject to **"cumulative disadvantage" or "compound risk"** Explain what this means and why it is a cause for concern.

37. Moderate a class discussion of **the Lionel Tate case**.

38. Invite a local juvenile probation officer to address your class regarding factors he or she considers when **making a decision to violate a probationer**. (Community Corrections and Probation)

39. Invite a local juvenile court judge to address your class regarding factors he or she considers when making a decision **to waive jurisdiction** of a juvenile offender to criminal court. (Courts)


## Women

1. Visit a local **community corrections center for women**. Discuss with the women the problems they are having in adjusting and what they think can be done to alleviate them. (Community Corrections and Probation)

2. Arrange a tour of a women's prison. Have the students discuss with the staff the **differences they think are present between women's prison and men's prisons**. Finally, require the students to write an essay that highlights these differences. (Incarceration and Prison Society)

3. Have the director of corrections in the state come to class and discuss the **purpose of female prisons**. Examine how programming is different for women when compared to men. Have the class explore the justifications for these differences with the director. (Incarceration and Prison Society)

4. Contact the office of public information in your state capital and request a copy of the state budget that outlines the amount of **money spent on corrections for men and women**. Is there a

difference? Is the difference proportionate to the number of men and women incarcerated? (Community Corrections and Probation)

5. Discuss the many **ways that African-Americans and women have been discriminated against in policing**. (Race)

6. You have been appointed the Personnel Director of the City of Anywhere, U.S.A. Anywhere, with a population of 60,000 has a police department of 120 officers. There are currently no female officers on the department, and the department is expected to lose 30 officers through retirement this year. The local chapter of the National Organization of Women (NOW) is claiming that Anywhere is discriminating against females in its police hiring process. Develop a comprehensive plan to **increase female representation in the department.** (Policing)

7. Have the students examine the **differences between females and males in their levels of criminal involvement**. Find, or develop, a list of about 50 delinquent acts including alcohol and drug use, minor criminal acts, and more serious criminal acts. Hand this form out to the students. They are to mark on the form whether they are female or male and each item they committed prior to the age of 18. Have them turn these forms in and then redistribute them to the class. On the board, write two sets of 1-50 (one for male sheets and one for female sheets). Have the students place on the board a check mark next to the items that are marked on their sheet. Taking into account the gender distribution within your class, discuss those items where females and males report similar levels of offending and those items where there is a clear disparity. (Criminology)

8. Invite a representative from the National Organization for Women (NOW) to discuss **female crime in the 21st Century.**

9. Arrange to have the class visit **a local jail** and observe if there is a separation of males and females and boys and girls. (Juvenile Justice)

10. Have the students review the **T.V. Guide listings** for the last five years during prime time. Track how many shows are dominated by females and how many are dominated by males. Have them keep track of how many have a female title. Discuss the implications.

# CHAPTER 9

# CAREERS

## Careers

1. Explain to the students how you developed an interest in the field of criminal justice, and why you decided to go into the area of **teaching criminal justice**.

2. Invite members from your **local criminal justice community** to come to class and discuss their jobs, as well as internships their agencies might have available. (Criminal Justice)

3. Invite a **DEA agent** to class to discuss the role of the DEA in controlling the drug trade. (Drugs)

4. Academy of Criminal Justice Sciences (www.acjs.org): Encourage students to examine the link to **student scholarships and awards**.

5. Invite a member of **the FBI** to come to class to discuss the new mission of the FBI. (Terrorism and Homeland Security)

6. Invite local representatives of the **various law enforcement agencies** discussed in the text to come to class and discuss their jobs. (Policing)

7. Divide the class into small groups. Have each group develop a list of qualifications for **the "ideal" police officer**. (Policing)

8. Invite police officers from several surrounding agencies to come to class and discuss the **qualifications required by their departments**, as well as salaries and advancement possibilities (e.g., how long does it take the average person to become a detective in each department?). (Policing)

9. Invite some **female police officers** to come to class and frankly discuss the issues they face as women in a traditionally male-oriented profession. (Policing)

10. Develop a research paper on the **"Women in Policing."** (Policing)

11. Find out what kinds of qualifications are required for particular types of **judges** in your state. Engage students in a discussion of these qualifications. (Courts)

12. Have students put together a list of qualifications for **the "ideal" judge**. (Courts)

13. Invite **a prosecutor and a defense attorney** to come to class and discuss their occupations. This is an especially effective activity if one of them is a former graduate of your program. (Courts)

14. Invite a **probation officer** to come to class and discuss his or her job duties. (Community Corrections and Probation)

15. Find out the qualifications required for **correctional officers** at the nearest prison. Have the students discuss their qualifications. Encourage student discussion of this occupation. Do any of them want to be a prison guard? Why or why not? (Incarceration and Prison Society)

16. Invite **a parole officer** to come to class to discuss his or her job duties. See if it is possible for her or her to bring a parolee along. ? (Incarceration and Prison Society)

17. Have students interview **guards in a jail or prison** and develop a paper on guarding the institution based on these interviews. (Incarceration and Prison Society)

18. Invite **a juvenile probation officer** to come to class and discuss his or her job duties. Also have the probation officer discuss internship opportunities available for your students. (Community Corrections and Probation, Juvenile Justice)

19. Interview a **practitioner** who actually works in the criminal justice field and give a 10-minute class report about the interview. Include a table of the organization of the practitioner's agency, the practitioner's opinion about the system, their career advice, their day-to-day activities on the job, and their opinion of the job. (Criminal Justice)

20. Using the web, access ten **job descriptions** of people working in the criminal justice system. (Criminal Justice)

21. Right now, it is not generally necessary to **have highly educated (formal education) correctional officers**. Administrators often claim that all that is needed is training. What is your opinion about this issue? Are you in favor of increased education or not? Please include in your response the difference between education and training. Please give your opinion in a 1,500 word essay using data and cite the sources for all data used. (Corrections)

22. Have the students interview a **police officer**. Require the students report on the organization of the police department as well as its bureaucracy. (Policing)

23. Have a number of students participate in **ride along with local police** and then have them report their experiences to the entire class. What did the students learn about police response and action from the ride along? Did it change their perception of work at all? How? (Policing)

24. Exercise: **Recruitment and Training of Police Officers** (Policing)

    a.  What qualifications would you require for someone to be hired as a police officer? Why?

    b.  What salary and benefits would you offer in order to attract the police officer-candidates that you described?

    c.  What are the three most important subjects that should be taught to new police recruits? Why?

    d.  Could you use training to combat any negative aspects of the police subculture and working personality? If so, how?

25. Students are always interested in the **career opportunities** available in the criminal justice system. There are a wide range of professionals involved at various stages of the process. Assign students one of these professions to investigate and then report back to the class. Students should gather information on such topics as educational requirements, starting salary, opportunities for mobility, job description, skills required, contact information, job market status, working conditions, etc.

# SOURCES

Armstrong, G. (2005). *Instructor's Guide for Walker, Spohn, and DeLone's The Color of Justice: Race, Ethnicity, and Crime in America* (4th ed.). Belmont, CA: Wadsworth Publishing Company.

Brinkley, S. (2006). *Instructor's Guide for Maxfield and Babbie's Basics of Research Methods.* Belmont, CA: Wadsworth Publishing Company.

Conley, E. (2006). *Instructor's Guide for White's Terrorism and Homeland Security* (5th ed). Belmont, CA: Wadsworth Publishing Company.

DeJong, C. (2007). *Instructor's Guide for Cole and Smith's The American System of Criminal Justice* (11th ed.). Belmont, CA: Wadsworth Publishing Company.

Heath-Thornton, D. (2005). *Instructor's Guide for Dempsey and Forst's An Introduction to Policing* (3rd ed.). Belmont, CA: Wadsworth Publishing Company.

Kessler, R.G. (2005). *Instructor's Guide for Neubauer's American Courts and the Criminal Justice System* (8th ed.). Belmont, CA: Wadsworth Publishing Company.

Kessler, R.G. (2005). *Instructor's Guide for Samaha's Criminal Law* (8th ed.). Belmont, CA: Wadsworth Publishing Company.

Lemley, E.C. (2006). *Instructor's Guide for Clear, Cole, and Reisig's American Corrections* (7th ed.). Belmont, CA: Wadsworth Publishing Company.

McAninch, T., & McAninch, H. (2005). *Instructor's Guide for Siegel, Welsh and Senna's Juvenile Delinquency: Theory, Practice, and Law* (9th ed.). Belmont, CA: Wadsworth Publishing Company.

Nees, H. (2007). *Instructor's Guide for Bennett and Hess's Criminal Investigation* (8th ed.). Belmont, CA: Wadsworth Publishing Company.

Newhart, L. (2007). *Instructor's Guide for Siegel and Senna's Essentials of Criminal Justice* (5th ed.). Belmont, CA: Wadsworth Publishing Company.

Pollock, J. (2007). *Instructor's Guide for Pollock's Ethical Dilemmas and Decisions in Criminal Justice* (5th ed.). Belmont, CA: Wadsworth Publishing Company.

Stone. M.K. (2005). *Instructor's Guide for Miller and Hess's Community Policing: Partnerships for Problem Solving* (4th ed.). Belmont, CA: Wadsworth Publishing Company.

Stone, M.K. (2006). *Instructor's Guide for Hess and Wrobleski's Police Operations: Theory and Practice* (4th ed.). Belmont, CA: Wadsworth Publishing Company.

Struckoff, D. (2007). *Instructor's Guide for Gaines and Miller's Criminal Justice in Action* (4th ed.). Belmont, CA: Wadsworth Publishing Company.

Wilson, J.K. (2006). *Instructor's Resource Manual for Siegel's Criminology* (9th ed.). Belmont, CA: Wadsworth Publishing Company.